THE ACADEMIC LIBRARY

BUDGET & EXPENDITURE REPORT

1999 EDITION

Primary Research Group, Inc. Tel:212-764-1579
isbn#: 1-57440-016-9

Primary Research Group, Inc.
68 West 38th Street, Suite #202
New York, New York 10018
Phone: 212-764-1579
Fax: 212-302-6530
isbn#: 1-57440-016-9

Primary Research Group, Inc.   **68 W. 38th St., #202, NY, NY 10018**   **(212)764-1579**

TABLE OF CONTENTS

Primary Research Group, Inc.   **68 W. 38th St., #202, NY, NY 10018**   **(212)764-1579**

2

List of Tables

Primary Research Group, Inc.   **68 W. 38th St., #202, NY, NY 10018**   **(212)764-1579**

Primary Research Group, Inc.   68 W. 38th St., #202, NY, NY 10018   (212)764-1579

13

Primary Research Group, Inc.   **68 W. 38th St., #202, NY, NY 10018**   **(212)764-1579**

THE ACADEMIC LIBRARY BUDGET & EXPENDITURE REPORT, 1999 EDITION

CHAPTER ONE: INTRODUCTION

SAMPLING STRATEGY

This study is based on a survey of 100 academic libraries chosen from a composite of directories especially arranged to overcome the limitations of any single directory. The survey was conducted by mail and by phone. Due to the sensitive nature of the some of the information, partial questionnaires were accepted from some participants. In addition to the formal phone and mail survey, Primary Research uses data from sources such as the U.S. Department of Education, the U.S. Department of Commerce, and state governments, among other sources.

Midway through the mail and phone survey, Primary Research staff performed a response pattern analysis to ascertain any response pattern biases. Some biases were detected (larger libraries tended to respond to mail surveys while smaller ones had a greater tendency to respond to phone surveys), and a specially stratified sample was then chosen to correct some of the response pattern biases. The finished product is based on the two samples -- a simple random sample chosen from among more than 3500 academic libraries in the United States & Canada -- and a second, stratified sample chosen from a more restricted universe of academic libraries in the United States & Canada that are also a subset of the first sample. The second sample was designed to help correct for any response pattern biases discovered in the initial simple random sample. Collection materials expenditure (or when this data was absent, total holdings) was used as a size criteria for measuring the size of the respondents and comparing it to the size of the overall population from which the sample was chosen. The overall population data was based on larger sample than the sample used for the actual data reported in the study. The second, targeted sample was arranged to increase the likelihood that under-represented libraries would be selected. Community colleges remain somewhat under-represented in the overall sample.

SAMPLE BREAK DOWN

The complete sample breaks down as follows:

Sample Broken Down By Type of College and Full Time Enrollment

Type of Library	Number in Sample
4-Year College/University	63
2-Year College	37

by Full Time Student Enrollment

Less than 2200	26
2201-3500	26
3501-7500	24
7501+	24

By Type of Control of the School

Public	53
Private	47

CHARACTERIZATION OF THE BREAK OUTS

In certain cases, Separate data is presented for community colleges, private colleges, 4-year colleges. **These categories are not completely mutually exclusive and do not account for the entire sample in various information categories.**

Community colleges are mostly 2-year institutions that offer associates degrees. 4-year public colleges are those which are sponsored by states, cities (provinces in the case of Canada) and other public government localities, or by the Federal Government of Canada. U.S. state universities account for most of this sample; a few colleges in the sample may receive much of their funding from local governments.

DEFINITION OF A LIBRARY

The libraries chosen for the study had to have a separate budget, as well as at least one full time or part-time person whose primary work responsibility was the maintenance of the library. All colleges that participated in the survey were accredited institutions. All were located in the United State or Canada.

UNIFORMITY OF DATA

The universe of colleges in the sample did not all answer all questions in the survey. In the survey, in many instances, Primary Research Group asked for three years worth of data; that is, data for the 1996-97 academic year, the 1997-98 academic year, and the 1998-99 academic year. Data for the 1998-99 academic year necessarily involved a degree of estimation, since most of the surveying was done in August, September and October of 1998. However, most libraries have a good idea of what they will spend their budgets on by the beginning of the academic year.

Not all schools provided three or even two years worth of data in a time series. Consequently, the universe of libraries that provided data for 1997-98 and 1998-99 is different from the universe of libraries that provided data for 1998-99 alone. In most cases, the difference is minor, amounting to fewer than four or five libraries out of a sample of one hundred. However, the basis for the data presented for individual types of information vehicles, such as commercial on-line services -- is the data from 1998-99 unless otherwise specified. This means that there can be slight discrepancies in the data that is compared by year and the data that is presented apart from considerations of yearly comparisons. The data presented for the purposes of yearly comparisons is drawn from the unviverse of libraries in the sample that gave data for both 1997-98 and for 1998-99. The data presented apart from considerations of yearly comparisons is drawn from a universe of libraries that gave data for 1998-99. Colleges that gave data for 1998-99 but not for 1997-98 would be included in the overall statistics but not in the comparative statistics.

SUMMARY OF AND COMMENTARY ON MAJOR FINDINGS

OVERALL SPENDING

Academic library spending increased an estimated 3.98% in 1998. In our last study, in 1996, academic library spending had increased by only 1.1% in that year.

BOOKS & DIRECTORIES

Book spending rose by 0.6% in nominal terms 1998 but our sample data suggests that book spending in real terms continued to decline by about 1.1%. The rate of decline in spending on books has slowed considerably. Between 1994 and 1996, spending in real terms for books by academic libraries fell an estimated 10%.

Mean spending for directories rose by less than 1% in nominal terms and actually fell by about 0.65% in real terms.

Only 8% of the libraries in the sample said that they would increase spending for print directories in the next year, while 26% said that they would reduce spending for print directories and 66% said that they would maintain their level of spending.

62.3% of all libraries will increase spending for accessing directories on-line.

JOURNALS

Academic library subscriptions to journals fell an estimates 2.33% in 1998-99. Our 1996 study found that journal subscriptions maintained had fallen by 2.42% in 1996, so the rate of decline in journal subscriptions appears to be remarkably steady.

Public colleges are cancelling more journal subscriptions than private colleges. In the sample, the mean number of journal subscriptions cancelled for the 1998-99 academic year was 67 for public colleges and 21 for private colleges.

Mean academic library spending for journals increased by 1.76%, from $227,850 in 1997-98 to $231,850 in 1998-99. That libraries are spending more for fewer journal subscriptions suggests, of course, that they are spending more *per* subscription. In fact, academic libraries are spending 4.18% more per journal subscription in 1998-99 than they did in 1997-98. Overall, spending on journals appears to have rebounded. Our 1996 study found that academic libraries were reducing journal spending by an estimated 7% in nominal terms.

DOCUMENT RETRIEVAL

The libraries in the sample increased document delivery services spending by more than 24%. This dramatic increase was largely due to the the substantial increase in usage by very large research-oriented college libraries. Fax and internet based document delivery services are displacing older ones based on courier delivery, and these new services probably account for most new usage.

CD-ROM

Spending increases for CD-ROM databases appears to have slowed; spending by the libraries in the sample rose by only 3.9%

Only 17% of academic libraries plan to increase the number of CD-ROM subscriptions that they maintain in the next year, while 26% plan to decrease the number of their CD-ROM subscriptions. Medium-sized and larger libraries account for most of the libraries that plan to reduce the number of CD-ROM subscriptions.

Our data suggests that the elasticity of demand for CD-ROM database subscriptions is high among small and large libraries. Respondents said that they would add an average of 2 workstations to their CD-ROM licenses for every 20% reduction in price.

Only 8.6% of the libraries in the sample had a DVD player, though 16.5% plan to purchase one in the next year. Community college libraries are more likely to have DVD player (or to plan to purchase one) than the libraries of 4-year colleges.

COMMERCIAL ON-LINE SERVICES

Academic library spending for commercial on-line services rose by 15.7% in 1998-99. Our 1996 study found that academic library on-line service spending had increased an estimated 7.7% in 1996. Only 20% of libraries say that they have substituted internet usage for commercial on-line services though more than 60% of libraries say that they have accessed commercial databases through the internet access option offered by commercial database vendors. The data seems to suggest that the internet is slowly becoming a pathway to the for-fee commercial database world, rather than a competitor to it.

AUDIO-VIDEO MATERIALS

Audio materials spending by the libraries in the sample rose by 5.89% in 1998-99, with 4-year colleges accounting for almost all of the increase in spending. Video materials spending by the libraries in the sample rose by 12.67% in 1998-99.

LIBRARY CATALOG

89% of college libraries make their catalog available on-line while about 14.4% make it available in a CD-ROM format.

About 73% of the libraries in the sample make their catalog available on the world-wide web.

An estimated 18% of academic libraries are planning to purchase a new cataloging system within the next year and 41.2% plan to purchase a new one within 3 years.

Only 16.3% of all academic libraries, predominantly those serving schools with less than 2200 students, make their card catalog available in paper format.

13.3% of the libraries in the sample outsource cataloging to a third party (not an employee of the library).

16% of the libraries in the sample outsource authority control.

LIBRARY SOFTWARE, COMPUTERS AND WORKSTATIONS

85% of academic libraries have an integrated software library system.

53.6% of academic libraries offer workstations equipped with applications software such as word processing, spreadsheets or statistical software.

41.46% of academic libraries plan to offer "holistic" workstations that offer both applications software and information services to patrons.

Academic libraries reduced new purchases of personal computers by 20% in the 1998-99 academic year, from a mean of 15 per library in 1997-98 to a mean of 12 in 1998-99.

IMPACT OF THE INTERNET

34.2% of academic libraries plan to increase their use of CD-ROM's as a means of database retrieval, while 64.56% plan to increase use of commercial on-line databases and 97.4% plan to increase the use of the internet as a pathway to database retrieval. Only 2.53% plan to increase use of databases accessed through magnetic tape.

Interestingly, while the internet is substituting for some commercial on-line usage, it appears that the internet's impact on commercial on-line services may very well be a favorable one in the academic library market, at least in the short term. Academic libraries are simply more and more aware of the on-line world in general, leading them to use both the internet and commercial on-line services more extensively.

ACADEMIC LIBRARIES AS A BELLWETHER FOR SOCIETY

Academic libraries have in part turned the corner on the very difficult financial circumstances that plagued them in the 1980's and early and mid 1990's when the share of general higher education revenues spent on libraries declined significantly.

After a long period of declines in spending in real terms, academic libraries are once again increasing their budgets. However, their spending increases still lag behind general economic growth by more than 1%. Many academic libraries still face declining or stagnant budgets, even in the face of rising enrollment. However, a minority of libraries is experiencing significant budget increases, mostly as a result of decisions to make major investments in on-line information. The decision to increase spending in this area is sometimes supported by college administrations anxious to bring the college "up to snuff" or "on the leading edge" in information technology applications. It now appears to be accepted by many college administrators that information technology investments pay off in the ways that administators expect: it helps to bring in students, business support, and generally increases the prestige of the institution.

The data in this report, and in our last study of academic libraries in 1996 shows that academic libraries, perhaps more than other institutions of society, have embraced the telecommunications revolution. The internet is becoming the major platform through which libraries access information, more important than CD-ROM, magnetic tape, commercial on-line services, computer disks and eventually even print media. Academic libraries are beginning to deal with information suppliers in a way that many computer industry forecasters suspect that the rest of America soon will: they are buying it over the internet.

CHANGING NATURE OF THE DATABASE MARKET

One of the great fears of database vendors has been that free information available over the internet would reduce their sales. This has not really happened. Although government information is often freely accessed over the internet, the quality and even the volume of information available for free over the internet does not approach what is available from fee-based on line services. However, the dramatic impact of the internet has been to reduce the bargaining power of brokers of database services and increase the bargaining power of consumers (in this case librarians) and of the producers of database services. For the producers, it is now easier to sell their information on-line directly to the consumer librarians, without having to go through a "middle-man" on-line service. The reduced bargaining power of the "middle-man" broker services can lead to lower prices, and to a restructuring of the on-line services industry.

Librarians are now dealing directly with several database companies, rather than with just one or two on-line broker services. Consequently, the bargaining power of the librarians has increased, since the database producers are smaller and more vulnerable to buying cooperatives and consortiums put together by the libraries. Also, the producers, able to offer their databases directly over the internet, often through easy-to-use search engines and interfaces, can better tailor their offerings to their audience, and better afford to charge lower prices. Libraries have also become savvy about joining consortiums and forcing both flat-rate and fee-based price concessions from vendors, both producers and brokers.

The internet-based restructuring of the on-line industry has been a major factor in driving down the real cost of information, increasing sales and encouraging libraries to substitute on-line information, particularly fee-based on-line services accessed through the internet, for information from print sources (except magazines) and CD-ROM. Fax based document retrieval services that offer internet access options have also become a major factor in the library market, especially for larger research libraries. It is not difficult to argue that academic library productivity, measured as the number of students and faculty served, and the extent of service, has significantly increased over the past ten years, but the fruits of increased productivity had in general not been reinvested back into academic libraries. In general, academic libraries have been able to increase productivity through automation but have been used as something like an academic "cash cows". In business, a cash cow is a product line whose success subsidizes the development of less-established products. Automation of academic libraries has allowed college administrations to reduce spending on libraries in real terms while enrollments (and presumably library usage) increased.

Our suspicion, however, is that 1998-99 may mark a turning point. Colleges are once again investing in their libraries. Between 1996 and 1998, many library purchasing trends remained the same. In 1995, the academic libraries in the sample reduced spending on computers, although spending on for on-line services, as they did in 1998. As expected, the reduction in hardware spending combined with continued strong interest in increasing spending on databases meant that academic libraries were fertile ground for an expected shift in the computer industry towards the delivery of content and applications programs from remote locations. At least in the highly wired academic library environment of the late 1990's, libraries are choosing to invest in telecommunications, in databases delivered from remote locations, rather than from the desktop.

In many respects, academic libraries serve as a early warning system or weather vane for the direction of change in information technologies for the broader society. The highly wired campus environment stimulates progress in information technologies.

The academic library environment is characterized by very high levels of information demand and, at least at the major research libraries, information-savvy consumers. A much higher percentage of the clientele of academic libraries have computers, CD-ROM's and modems than the population in the broader society. With the possible exception of large business firms involved in communications and information-oriented businesses, no groups of institutions process as much copyright information in such a compressed time frame as academic libraries. Many businesses have "information centers" but a major university is composed virtually exclusively of such centers of high information demand. The technology verdict from academic libraries is a critical indicator of the success of information technologies in the broader society. If this is the case, the internet is clearly emerging as the "operating system of the future". The ease of use of the library internet operating platform should be enhanced as voice recognition technologies become standard features of internet software.

Academic libraries will benefit tremendously from the new voice recognition technologies, which may allow patrons to search library collections by voice, bypassing the often tedious on-line systems. Additionally, voice-activated internet use may find its first application in the academic library. For the typical internet user at home or office, who may tap into the internet once or twice a day to retrieve e-mail or to conduct a quick search, voice recognition technology may save a few minutes. For an academic library using an internet-based platform to access databases, library collections and (probably soon) applications software, voice recognition technology is an extraordinary labor saving application, vastly increasing library search capabilities.

CHAPTER TWO: OVERALL SPENDING

TOTAL AND COMPENSATION SPENDING

Table #1: Total Mean Academic Library Spending, 1997-98 and 1998-99 ($ in thousand)

Year	Mean Spending	Median Spending	Minimum	Maximum	Percent Mean Increase
1997-98	$1244.9	650	30	12,000	
1998-99	$1294.5	659	35	12,500	3.98

Mean total spending for academic libraries that gave spending data for both 1997-98 and 1998-99 were $1,244,878 and $1,294,488 respectively. Our data suggests that academic library spending will grow a shade less than 4% in nominal terms in the 1998-99 academic year, about 2.5% in real terms, assuming a national inflation rate of 1.5%. This represents much faster budget growth than in recent years.

Indeed, our last report (The Academic Library Budget & Expenditure Report, 1996) found that academic library spending in real terms had fallen by 4.5% over the two year period 1995 and 1996. So, the apparent turn-around is extraordinary and far exceeds the increase in the growth rate of the economy, or the growth rate of academic enrollment.

However, the surge in spending does not appear to be very uniform. In our sample, median spending by academic libraries rose only from $650,000 to $659,000 in nominal terms, or by 1.38%. In real terms, median academic library spending is not even quite keeping pace with the Nation's modest rate of inflation. The robust overall growth rate in spending is most likely coming from a minority of academic libraries.

Table #2: Total Mean Academic Library Spending, Broken out by Type of Control of the School, Public or Private, 1997-98 ($ in thousand)

Type of Control	Mean Spending	Median Spending	Minimum	Maximum
Public	1,597.84	725.00	65.00	12,000.00
Private	934.82	599.55	30.00	6,300.00

Table #3: Total Mean Academic Library Spending, Broken out by Level of the School, Two-Year or Four-Year, 1997-98 ($ in thousand)

Level of the School	Mean Spending	Median Spending	Minimum	Maximum
Two-Year	546.62	458.03	30.00	1,704.72
Four-Year	1,709.17	935.75	93.00	12,000.00

Table #4: Total Mean Academic Library Spending, Broken out by Size of the School, 1997-98 ($ in thousand)

Size of the School	Mean Spending	Median Spending	Minimum	Maximum
1-2200	326.55	227.44	30.00	1,217.00
2201-3500	866.75	650.00	108.00	2,227.52
3501-7750	1,154.83	822.00	65.00	7,478.50
7751 and Above	3,068.56	2,100.00	457.17	12,000.00

Table #5: Total Mean Academic Library Spending, Broken out by Type of Control of the School, Public or Private, 1998-99 ($ in thousand)

Type of Control	Mean Spending	Median Spending	Minimum	Maximum
Public	1,582.77	775.00	65.00	12,500.00
Private	951.66	600.00	35.00	7,000.00

Table #6: Total Mean Academic Library Spending, Broken out by Level of the School, Two-Year or Four-Year, 1998-99 ($ in thousands)

Level of the School	Mean Spending	Median Spending	Minimum	Maximum
Two-Year	595.75	500.00	35.00	1,738.81
Four-Year	1,727.71	787.30	97.00	12,500.00

Table #7: Total Mean Academic Library Spending, Broken out by Size of the School, 1998-99 ($ in thousand)

Size of the School	Mean Spending	Median Spending	Minimum	Maximum
1-2200	284.40	215.00	35.00	980.00
2201-3500	840.80	682.50	110.00	2,221.17
3501-7750	797.56	604.64	65.00	2,500.00
7751 and Above	3,210.67	2,100.00	457.17	12,500.00

Spending on Salaries represent a mean of 45.28% of the academic libraries in the sample, with a median of 50%.

Table #8: Mean Percentage of Total Spending Accounted for by Salaries and other Compensation

	Mean Percentage	Median Percentage	Minimum	Maximum
All Libraries	45.28	50.00	0.00	85.00

Table #9: Mean Percentage of Total Spending Accounted for by Salaries and other Compensation, Broken out by Type of Control of the School, Public or Private

	Mean Percentage	Median Percentage	Minimum	Maximum
Public	49.67	54.90	0.00	85.00
Private	40.13	48.00	0.00	71.00

Table #10: Mean Percentage of Total Spending Accounted for by Salaries and other Compensation, Broken out by Level of the School, Two-Year or Four-Year

	Mean Percentage	Median Percentage	Minimum	Maximum
Two-Year	49.49	59.00	0.00	85.00
Four-Year	42.58	48.00	0.00	71.00

Table #11: Mean Percentage of Total Spending Accounted for by Salaries and other Compensation, Broken out by Size of the School

Size of the School	Mean Percentage	Median Percentage	Minimum	Maximum
1-2200	42.03	50.00	0.00	69.00
2201-3500	41.65	46.83	0.00	73.00
3501-7750	44.33	48.00	0.00	76.00
7751 and Above	53.86	58.00	0.00	85.00

CHAPTER THREE: BOOKS AND DIRECTORIES

Book spending grew by only 0.6% in nominal terms and actually fell in real terms. In real terms book spending fell about 1.1% in 1998. However, our last study found that book spending by academic libraries had fallen an average of about 3.33% per year in real terms from 1994 to 1996. Spending for directories also fell in real terms but librarians noted that they were accessing directories more on-line.

Table #12: Total Mean Academic Library Book Spending, 1997-98 and 1998-99 ($ in thousands)

	Mean Spending	Median Spending	Minimum	Maximum	Percent Mean Increase
1997-98	$159.8	90.00	50	1500	
1998-99	$160.8	87.55	50	1400	0.6%

Table #13: Mean Academic Library Book Spending, Broken out by Type of Control of the School, Public or Private, 1998-99 ($ in thousands)

Type of Control	Mean Spending	Median Spending	Minimum	Maximum
Public	176.88	68.50	3.50	1,400.00
Private	140.34	90.00	0.05	552.00

Table #14: Mean Academic Library Book Spending, Broken out by Level of the School, Two-Year or Four-Year, 1998-99 ($ in thousands)

Level of the School	Mean Spending	Median Spending	Minimum	Maximum
Two-Year	84.53	49.98	4.30	475.00
Four-Year	203.27	122.00	0.05	1,400.00

Table #15: Mean Academic Library Book Spending, Broken out by Size of the School, 1998-99 ($ in thousands)

Size of the School	Mean Spending	Median Spending	Minimum	Maximum
1-2200	65.23	52.50	3.50	386.00
2201-3500	138.79	113.75	17.00	402.10
3501-7750	135.75	123.50	0.05	475.00
7751 and Above	304.53	165.00	4.30	1,400.00

Table #16: Mean Academic Library Book Spending, Broken out by Type of Control of the School, Public or Private, 1997-98 ($ in thousands)

Type of Control	Mean Spending	Median Spending	Minimum	Maximum
Public	203.79	69.69	0.50	1,500.00
Private	152.48	115.00	0.05	666.00

Table 17: Mean Academic Library Book Spending, Broken out by Level of the School, Two-Year or Four-Year, 1997-98 ($ in thousands)

Level of the School	Mean Spending	Median Spending	Minimum	Maximum
Two-Year	69.08	47.30	0.50	475.00
Four-Year	247.04	143.96	0.05	1,500.00

Table #18: Mean Academic Library Book Spending, Broken out by Size of the School, 1997-98 ($ in thousands)

Size of the School	Mean Spending	Median Spending	Minimum	Maximum
1-2200	62.56	47.50	4.20	375.00
2201-3500	127.46	110.00	6.67	372.76
3501-7750	206.22	133.25	0.05	1,080.96
7751 and Above	347.77	196.41	4.30	1,500.00

Table #19: Total Mean Academic Library Directory Spending, 1997-98 and 1998-99 ($ in thousands)

	Mean Spending	Median Spending	Minimum	Maximum	Percent Mean Increase
1997-98	$12.87	4.25	0	80	
1998-99	$12.98	4.32	0	80	0.85%

Mean spending for directories rose by less than 1% in nominal terms and actually fell by about 0.85% in real terms.

Table #20: Mean Academic Library Directory Spending, Broken out by Type of Control of the School, Public or Private, 1997-98 ($ in thousands)

Type of Control	Mean Spending	Median Spending	Minimum	Maximum
Public	8.70	1.68	0.00	80.00
Private	9.44	4.50	0.00	50.00

Table #21: Mean Academic Library Directory Spending, Broken out by Level of the School, Two-Year or Four-Year, 1997-98 ($ in thousands)

Level of the School	Mean Spending	Median Spending	Minimum	Maximum
Two-Year	5.01	2.00	0.00	20.00
Four-Year	12.82	2.93	0.00	80.00

Table #22: Mean Academic Library Directory Spending, Broken out by Size of the School, 1997-98 ($ in thousands)

Size of the School	Mean Spending	Median Spending	Minimum	Maximum
1-2200	1.56	0.75	0.00	5.50
2201-3500	4.80	4.00	0.00	19.00
3501-7750	7.50	7.50	7.50	7.50
7751 and Above	25.25	10.75	0.00	80.00

Table #23: Mean Academic Library Directory Spending, Broken out by Type of Control of the School, Public or Private, 1998-99 ($ in thousands)

Type of Control	Mean Spending	Median Spending	Minimum	Maximum
Public	13.07	2.05	0.00	80.00
Private	12.83	6.00	3.50	50.00

Table #24: Mean Academic Library Directory Spending, Broken out by Level of the School, Two-Year or Four-Year, 1998-99 ($ in thousands)

Level of the School	Mean Spending	Median Spending	Minimum	Maximum
Two-Year	6.52	2.75	0.50	21.00
Four-Year	19.45	6.00	0.00	80.00

Table #25: Mean Academic Library Directory Spending, Broken out by Size of the School, 1998-99 ($ in thousands)

Size of the School	Mean Spending	Median Spending	Minimum	Maximum
1-2200	1.83	1.50	0.00	4.00
2201-3500	7.95	5.00	2.10	21.00
3501-7750	7.50	7.50	7.50	7.50
7751 and Above	37.38	34.00	1.50	80.00

Note: only about a fifth of the libraries in the sample tracked their spending on directories, so the response rate to this question was much lower than for all other questions.

Table #26: Percentage of Academic Libraries that Plan to Increase, Decrease, and Maintain the Same Spending on Print Directories in the Next Two Years

	Increase	Stay the Same	Decrease
All Libraries	8.2%	65.6%	26.2%

Table #27: Percentage of Academic Libraries that Plan to Increase, Decrease, and Maintain the Same Spending on Print Directories in the Next Two Years, Broken out by Type of Control of the School, Public or Private

Type of Control	Increase	Stay the Same	Decrease
Private	10.7%	57.1%	32.1%
Public	6.1%	72.7%	21.2%

Table #28: Percentage of Academic Libraries that Plan to Increase, Decrease, and Maintain the Same Spending on Print Directories in the Next Two Years, Broken out by Level of the School, Two-Year or Four-Year

Level of the School	Increase	Stay the Same	Decrease
Four-Year	7.70%	59.1%	33.3%
Two-Year	9.10%	77.3%	13.6%

Table #29: Percentage of Academic Libraries that Plan to Increase, Decrease, and Maintain the Same Spending on Print Directories in the Next Two Years, Broken out by Size of the School

Size of the School	Increase	Stay the Same	Decrease
2200 and Less	10.5%	78.9%	10.5%
2201 - 3500	13.3%	53.3%	33.3%
3501 - 7750	7.7%	69.2%	23.1%
7751 and Above	0.0%	57.1%	42.9%

Table #30: Percentage of Academic Libraries that Plan to Increase, Decrease, and Maintain the Same Sending on CD-ROM Directories in the Next Two Years

	Increase	Stay the Same	Decrease
All Libraries	33.3%	43.35%	23.3%

Table #31: Percentage of Academic Libraries that Plan to Increase, Decrease, and Maintain the Same Sending on CD-ROM Directories in the Next Two Years, Broken out by Type of Control of the School, Public or Private

Type of Control	Increase	Stay the Same	Decrease
Public	45.5%	39.4%	15.2%
Private	18.5%	48.1%	33.3%

Table #32: Percentage of Academic Libraries that Plan to Increase, Decrease, and Maintain the Same Sending on CD-ROM Directories in the Next Two Years, Broken Out by Level of the School, Two-Year or Four-Year

Level of the School	Increase	Stay the Same	Decrease
Four-Year	21.6%	51.4%	27.0%
Two-Year	50.0%	31.8%	18.2%

Table #33: Percentage of Academic Libraries that Plan to Increase, Decrease, and Maintain the Same Spending on CD-ROM Directories in the Next Two Years, Broken out by Size of the School

Size of the School	Increase	Stay the Same	Decrease
2200 and Less	29.4%	47.1%	23.5%
2201 - 3500	25.0%	43.8%	31.3%
3501 - 7750	38.5%	46.2%	15.4%
7751 and Above	38.5%	38.5%	23.1%

Table #34: Percentage of Academic Libraries that Plan to Increase, Decrease, and Maintain the Same Spending on Directories accessed through Commercial On-Line Services in the Next Two Years

	Increase	Stay the Same	Decrease
All Libraries	62.3%	34.0%	3.8%

Table #35: Percentage of Academic Libraries that Plan to Increase, Decrease, and Maintain the Same Spending on Directories accessed through Commercial On-Line Services in the Next Two Years, Broken out by Type of Control of the School, Public or Private

Type of Control	Increase	Stay the Same	Decrease
Public	64.3%	32.1%	3.6%
Private	60.0%	36.0%	4.0%

Table #36: Percentage of Academic Libraries that Plan to Increase, Decrease, and Maintain the Same Spending on Directories accessed through Commercial On-Line Services in the Next Two Years, Broken out by Level of the School, Two-Year or Four-Year

Level of the School	Increase	Stay the Same	Decrease
Two-Year	61.11%	33.33%	5.56%
Four-Year	62.86%	34.29%	2.86%

* Note: Numbers may not add up to 100.00 due to rounding

Table #37: Percentage of Academic Libraries that Plan to Increase, Decrease, and Maintain the Same Spending on Directories accessed through Commercial On-Line Services in the Next Two Years, Broken out by Size of the School

Size of the School	Increase	Stay the Same	Decrease
2200 and Less	56.25%	31.25%	12.50%
2201 - 3500	46.15%	53.85%	0.00%
3501 - 7750	72.73%	27.27%	0.00%
7751 and Above	76.92%	23.08%	0.00%

Table #38: Percentage of Academic Libraries that Plan to Increase, Decrease, and Maintain the Same Spending on Directories accessed through the Web Pages of Directory Publishers in the next Two Years

	Increase	Stay the Same	Decrease
All Libraries	75.00%	25.00%	0.00%

Table #39: Percentage of Academic Libraries that Plan to Increase, Decrease, and Maintain the Same Spending on Directories accessed through the Web Pages of Directory Publishers in the next Two Years, Broken out by Type of Control of the School, Public or Private

Type of Control	Increase	Stay the Same	Decrease
Public	68.00%	32.00%	0.00%
Private	81.48%	18.52%	0.00%

Table #40: Percentage of Academic Libraries that Plan to Increase, Decrease, and Maintain the Same Spending on Directories accessed through the Web Pages of Directory Publishers in the next Two Years, Broken out by Level of the School, Two-Year or Four-Year

Level of the School	Increase	Stay the Same	Decrease
Two-Year	82.35%	17.65%	0.00%
Four-Year	71.43%	28.57%	0.00%

Table #41: Percentage of Academic Libraries that Plan to Increase, Decrease, and Maintain the Same Spending on Directories accessed through the Web Pages of Directory Publishers in the next Two Years, Broken out by Size of the School

Size of the School	Increase	Stay the Same	Decrease
1-2200	68.75%	31.25%	0.00%
2201-3500	78.57%	21.43%	0.00%
3501-7750	75.00%	25.00%	0.00%
7751 and Above	80.00%	20.00%	0.00%

CHAPTER FOUR: JOURNALS

Academic libraries continued to reduce the number of their journal holdings, at about the same rate as they have over the past four or five years, that is, by about 2.2 to 2.5% of titles per year. At the same time, the mean academic library spending for journals increased by 1.76%, from $227,850 in 1997-98 to $231,850 in 1998-99. That the libraries are spending more for fewer journal subscriptions suggests, of course, that they are spending more *per* subscription. As the following table illustrates, academic libraries are spending 4.18% more per journal subscription in 1998-99 than they did in 1997-98.

Table #42: Total Number of Journal Subscriptions Maintained by Academic Libraries, 1997-98 and 1998-99

	Mean Number	Median Number	Minimum	Maximum	Percent Mean Increase
1997-98	$1588	600	0	19003	
1998-99	$1551	600	30	19000	-2.33%

For the academic libraries that reported total number of journal subscriptions in both 1997-98 and 1998-99, the mean number of subscriptions was 1588 and 1551, respectively.

Table #43: Mean Number of Journal Subscriptions Maintained by Academic Libraries, Broken out by Type of Control of the School, Public or Private, 1997-98

Type of Control	Mean Number	Median Number	Minimum	Maximum
Public	1577	410	26	18,607
Private	1579	1000	0	19,003

Table #44: Mean Number of Journal Subscriptions Maintained by Academic Libraries, Broken out by Level of the School, Two-Year or Four-Year, 1997-98

Level of the School	Mean Number	Median Number	Minimum	Maximum
Two-Year	368	344	6	848
Four-Year	2316	1350	0	19,003

Table #45: Mean Number of Journal Subscriptions Maintained by Academic Libraries, Broken out by Size of the School, 1997-98

Size of the School	Mean Number	Median Number	Minimum	Maximum
1-2200	518	367	0	250
2201-3500	955	600	6	293
3501-7750	1,212	1,000	225	476
7751 and above	3,728	1,500	180	354

Table #46: Mean Number of Journal Subscriptions Maintained by Academic Libraries, Broken out by Type of Control of the School, Public or Private, 1998-99

Type of Control	Mean Number	Median Number	Minimum	Maximum
Public	1,798	410	78	19,000
Private	1,529	1,000	30	15,500

Table #47: Mean Number of Journal Subscriptions Maintained by Academic Libraries, Broken out by Level of the School, Two-Year or Four-Year, 1998-99

Level of the College	Mean Number	Median Number	Minimum	Maximum
Two-Year	375	350	125	800
Four-Year	2,491	1,342	30	1,900

Table #48: Mean Number of Journal Subscriptions Maintained by Academic Libraries, Broken out by Size of the School, 1998-99

Size of the School	Mean Number	Median Number	Minimum	Maximum
1-2200	525	360	30	1,898
2201-3500	918	455	125	2,725
3501-7750	1,525	1,000	225	10,747
7751 and above	3,591	1,740	180	19,000

Table #49: Total Mean Number of Journal Subscriptions that Academic Libraries Expect to Cancel in 1998-98

	Mean Number	Median Number	Minimum	Maximum
All Libraries	19	2	0	450

Table #50: Mean Number of Journal Subscriptions that Academic Libraries Expect to Cancel in 1998-99, Broken out by Type of Control of the School, Public or Private

Type of Control	Mean Number	Median Number	Minimum	Maximum
Public	17	3	0	100
Private	21	0	0	450

Table #51: Mean Number of Journal Subscriptions that Academic Libraries Expect to Cancel in 1998-98, Broken out by Level of the School, Two-Year or Four-Year

Level of the College	Mean Number	Median Number	Minimum	Maximum
Two-Year	14	2	0	100
Four-Year	22	1	0	450

Table #52: Mean Number of Journal Subscriptions that Academic Libraries Expect to Cancel in 1998-98, Broken out by Size of the School

Size of the School	Mean Number	Median Number	Minimum	Maximum
1-2200	5	0	0	28
2201-3500	8	0	0	67
3501-7750	19	5	0	69
7751 and Above	43	6	0	450

Table #53: Total Mean Number of Journal Subscriptions that Academic Libraries Expect to Add in 1998-99

	Mean Number	Median Number	Minimum	Maximum
All Libraries	17	5	0	400

Table #54: Mean Number of Journal Subscriptions that Academic Libraries Expect to Add in 1998-99, Broken out by Type of Control of the School, Public or Private

Type of Control	Mean Number	Median Number	Minimum	Maximum
Public	18	2	0	400
Private	17	5	0	200

Table #55: Mean Number of Journal Subscriptions that Academic Libraries Expect to Add in 1998-99, Broken out by Level of the School, Two-Year or Four-Year

Level of the School	Mean Spending	Median Spending	Minimum	Maximum
Two-Year	6	2	0	50
Four-Year	26	6	0	400

Table #56: Mean Number of Journal Subscriptions that Academic Libraries Expect to Add in 1998-99, Broken out by Size of the School

Size of the School	Mean Number	Median Number	Minimum	Maximum
1-2200	9	2	0	50
2201-3500	23	9	0	200
3501-7750	10	5	0	50
7751 and Above	28	1	0	400

Table #57: Total Mean Academic Library Journal Spending, 1997-98 and 1998-99 ($ in thousands)

	Mean Spending	Median Spending	Minimum	Maximum	Percent Mean Increase
1997-98	227.85	40.00	0.00	2,600.00	
1998-99	231.85	43.88	2.50	2,600.00	1.76%

Table #58: Mean Academic Library Journal Spending per Subscription, 1997-98 and 1998-99

	Mean Spending Per Subscription	Percent Mean Increase
1997-98	143.48	
1998-99	149.48	4.18%

Table #59: Mean Academic Library Journal Spending, Broken out by Type of Control of the School, Public or Private, 1997-98 ($ in thousands)

Type of Control	Mean Spending	Median Spending	Minimum	Maximum
Public	305.48	39.77	538	2,600.00
Private	224.53	87.55	0	2,624.57

Table #60: Mean Academic Library Journal Spending, Broken out by Level of the School, Two-Year or Four-Year, 1997-98 ($ in thousands)

Level of the School	Mean Spending	Median Spending	Minimum	Maximum
Two-Year	305.50	39.77	0.54	708.54
Four-Year	224.53	87.55	0.00	2,624.57

Table #61: Mean Academic Library Journal Spending, Broken out by Size of the School, 1997-98

Size of the School	Mean Spending	Median Spending	Minimum	Maximum
1-2200	50.10	35.00	0	10,435
2201-3500	110.55	40.00	538	16,774
3501-7750	221.80	85.00	9000	40,000
7751 and above	696.93	375.00	6500	35,000

Table #62: Mean Academic Library Journal Spending, Broken out by Type of Control of the School, Public or Private, 1998-99 ($ in thousands)

Type of Control	Mean Spending	Median Spending	Minimum	Maximum
Public	274.71	40.00	6.20	2,600.00
Private	182.87	85.00	2.50	1,700.00

Table #63: Mean Academic Library Journal Spending, Broken out by Level of the School, Two-Year or Four-Year, 1998-99 ($ in thousands)

Level of the School	Mean Spending	Median Spending	Minimum	Maximum
Two-Year	48.38	21.50	25.00	723.00
Four-Year	341.15	145.61	10.64	2,600.00

Table #64: Mean Academic Library Journal Spending, Broken out by Size of the School, 1998-99 ($ in thousands)

Size of the School	Mean Spending	Median Spending	Minimum	Maximum
1-2200	46.16	40.00	2.50	170.00
2201-3500	109.51	42.60	10.50	378.00
3501-7750	140.42	77.50	9.00	460.84
7751 and above	672.74	412.50	6.50	2,600.00

The 1998-99 academic year will see a significant increase in the mean number of non-journal print subscriptions maintained by academic libraries. The libraries will maintain a mean number of 238 non-journal print subscriptions, up 16.6% from the 1997-98 academic year, during which the libraries maintained 204 subscriptions.

Table #65: Total Mean Number of Non-Journal Print Subscriptions Maintained by Academic Libraries, 1997-98 and 1998-99

	Mean Number	Median Number	Minimum	Maximum	% Mean Increase
1997-98	204	45	0	624	
1998-99	238	45	0	1000	16.67

Table #66: Mean Number of Non-Journal Print Periodical Subscriptions Maintained by Academic Libraries, Broken out by Type of Control of the School, Public or Private, 1997-98

Type of Control	Mean Number	Median Number	Minimum	Maximum
Public	138	10	0	605
Private	319	322	7	624

Table #67: Mean Number of Non-Journal Print Periodical Subscriptions Maintained by Academic Libraries, Broken out by Level of the School, Two-Year or Four-Year, 1997-98

Level of the School	Mean Number	Median Number	Minimum	Maximum
Two-Year	67	28	0	200
Four-Year	369	600	7	624

Table #68: Mean Number of Non-Journal Print Periodical Subscriptions Maintained by Academic Libraries, Broken out by Size of the School, 1997-98

Size of the School	Mean Number	Median Number	Minimum	Maximum
1-2200	45	9	0	200
2201-3500	74	74	7	141
3501-7750	624	624	624	624
7751 and above	603	603	600	605

Table #69: Mean Number of Non-Journal Print Periodicals Maintained by Academic Libraries, Broken out by Type of Control of the School, Public or Private, 1998-99

Type of Control	Mean Number	Median Number	Minimum	Maximum
Public	135	10	0	585
Private	419	335	7	1000

Table #70: Mean Number of Non-Journal Print Periodicals Maintained by Academic Libraries, Broken out by Level of the School, Four-Year or Two-Year, 1998-99

Level of the School	Mean Number	Median Number	Minimum	Maximum
Two-Year	67	28	0	200
Four-Year	444	585	6	1000

Table #71: Mean Number of Non-Journal Print Periodicals Maintained by Academic Libraries, Broken out by Size of the School, 1998-99

Size of the School	Mean Number	Median Number	Minimum	Maximum
1-2200	44	8	0	200
2201-3500	74	74	7	141
3501-7750	624	624	624	624
7751 and above	793	793	585	1000

CHAPTER FIVE: DOCUMENT DELIVERY SERVICES

Estimated academic library spending for document delivery services rose by 24.53% in the 1998-99 academic year, as mean per library spending increased from $6,360 to $7,920. However, median spending was just one hundred and fifty dollars; many libraries spending almost nothing for document delivery services. The dramatic increase is due to vast increases by very large, mostly research-oriented colleges and universities, which have reduced journal subscriptions and often substituted document delivery. These research oriented colleges limit journal subscriptions but often circulate tables of contents to key faculty and allow them to order key articles.

Table #72: Total Mean Academic Library Document Delivery Services Spending, 1997-98 and 1998-99 ($ in thousands)

	Mean Spending	Median Spending	Minimum	Maximum	Percent Mean Increase
1997-98	6.36	0.10	0.00	150.00	
1998-99	7.92	0.15	0.00	200.00	24.53%

Table #73: Mean Academic Library Document Delivery Services Spending, Broken out by Type of Control of the School, Public or Private, 1997-98 ($ in thousands)

Type of Control	Mean Spending	Median Spending	Minimum	Maximum
Public	8.47	0.03	0.00	150.00
Private	4.07	0.37	0.00	600.00

Table #74: Mean Academic Library Document Delivery Services Spending, Broken out by Level of the School, Two-Year or Four-Year, 1997-98 ($ in thousands)

Level of the School	Mean Spending	Median Spending	Minimum	Maximum
Two-Year	0.33	0.00	0.00	3.00
Four-Year	10.16	0.86	0.00	150.00

Table #75: Mean Academic Library Document Delivery Services Spending, Broken out by Size of the School, 1997-98 ($ in thousands)

Size of the School	Mean Spending	Median Spending	Minimum	Maximum
1-2200	0.77	0.00	0.00	10.00
2201-3500	3.46	0.00	0.00	30.00
3501-7750	1.90	0.35	0.00	16.31
7751 and above	22.42	0.75	0.00	150.00

Table #76: Mean Academic Library Document Delivery Services Spending, Broken out by Type of Control of the School, 1998-99 ($ in thousands)

Type of Control	Mean Spending	Median Spending	Minimum	Maximum
Public	10.41	0.01	0.00	200.00
Private	4.84	0.43	0.00	54.00

Table #77: Mean Academic Library Document Delivery Service Spending, Broken out by Level of the School, Two-Year or Four-Year, 1998-99 ($ in thousands)

Level of the School	Mean Spending	Median Spending	Minimum	Maximum
Two-Year	0.41	0.00	0.00	4.00
Four-Year	13.26	1.10	0.00	200.00

Table #78: Mean Academic Library Document Delivery Service Spending, Broken out by Size of the School, 1998-99 ($ in thousands)

Size of the School	Mean Spending	Median Spending	Minimum	Maximum
1-2200	0.38	0.00	0.00	2.00
2201-3500	4.58	0.21	0.00	35.00
3501-7750	1.32	0.50	0.00	5.00
7751 and above	29.61	3.44	0.00	200.00

CHAPTER SIX: ON-LINE SERVICES

Academic library on-line services spending rose dramatically in 1998, as academic libraries continued to shift away from print and towards electronic media. However, academic libraries, especially larger ones, began to shift away from CD-ROM and more towards on-line services. The shift began in 1996 and has been accelerated by the internet-based access offered by many producers of on-line databases. In the past, many of these database vendors were compelled to offer their services through brokerage services, but now can offer their databases directly on-line through the internet. This development has increased the level of competition in the on-line industry, and enabled librarians to fine tune their information purchases, tailoring them more closely to their libraries actual needs. The increase in competition, combined with the apparent high elasticity of demand for on-line information, has led to lower prices for information accessed on line, and a boom in spending. The recovery of the US economy, increases in enrollment at the nation's colleges, and the increasing penetration of the personal computer and internet usage into the Nation's home (up from 33% to 45% over the past four years) has also stimulated academic library usage of on-line services.

As libraries gradually shift more fully to a networked environment, Primary Research Group expects on-line usage to continue to grow at double digit levels for the next three to four years, spurred by the following developments:

1) Networked CD-ROM's have assumed the role of-line services for many smaller colleges, particularly community colleges. However, over the next few years, Primary Research Group expects that telecommunications costs and other costs associated with internet-accessed databases will fall fast enough so that small colleges will begin to use telecom options to the detriment of CD-ROM. The major advance in CD-ROM technology -- DVD -- is a formidable achievement -- and will ultimately help rekindle library spending on audio/video materials, a trend that is already underway. But it will not offer the critical "drop by drop" information targeting that so many libraries need in an era of high prices for print information. The on-line world is extremely competitive as large and small database producers and brokers jockey for competitive advantage, in an environment with low cost entry barriers, and a tradition of relatively low brand loyalty.

In many respects, what is happening in academic libraries will happen to the rest of the world three to five years later. This has been the pattern over the past ten years. Major advances in computing and telecommunications happen in the information intensive environment of the academic library first. The on-line library catalog was one of the first institution-wide uses of distributed on-line information; the internet's first application was in academia; CD-ROM first caught on as a library research tool.

Table #79: Total Mean Academic Library On-Line Services Spending, 1997-98 and 1998-99 ($ in thousands)

	Mean Spending	Median Spending	Minimum	Maximum
1997-98	25.17	8.00	0.00	314.00
1998-99	29.09	11.00	0.00	408.00

Table #80: Mean Academic Library On-Line Services Spending, Broken out by Type of Control of the School, Public or Private, 1997-98 ($ in thousands)

Type of Control	Mean Spending	Median Spending	Minimum	Maximum
Public	21.23	5.00	0.00	202.87
Private	56.26	15.00	0.00	660.00

Table #81: Mean Academic Library On-Line Service Spending, Broken out by Level of the School, Two-Year or Four-Year, 1997-98 ($ in thousands)

Level of the School	Mean Spending	Median Spending	Minimum	Maximum
Two-Year	9.30	4.59	0.00	53.00
Four-Year	55.27	15.00	0.00	660.00

Table #82: Mean Academic Library On-Line Services Spending, Broken out by Size of the School, 1997-98 ($ in thousands)

Size of the School	Mean Spending	Median Spending	Minimum	Maximum
1-2200	10.85	3.90	0.00	50.00
2201-3500	30.12	8.99	0.00	150.00
3501-7750	46.40	8.00	0.00	660.00
7751 and above	59.57	27.50	0.00	314.00

Table #83: Mean Academic Library On-Line Services Spending, Broken out by Type of Control of the School, Public or Private, 1998-99 ($ in thousands)

Type of Control	Mean Spending	Median Spending	Minimum	Maximum
Public	19.96	10.00	0.00	179.82
Private	40.50	15.00	0.00	408.00

Table #84: Mean Academic Library On-Line Services Spending, Broken out by Level of the School, Two-Year or Four-Year, 1998-99 ($ in thousands)

Level of the School	Mean Spending	Median Spending	Minimum	Maximum
Two-Year	11.02	6.76	0.00	55.00
Four-Year	40.21	15.00	0.00	408.00

Table #85: Mean Academic Library On-Line Services Spending, Broken out by Size of the School ($ in thousands)

Size of the School	Mean Spending	Median Spending	Minimum	Maximum
1-2200	8.01	4.10	0.00	40.00
2201-3500	26.61	14.50	0.00	150.23
3501-7750	14.23	10.00	0.00	100.00
7751 and above	65.47	408.00	0.00	408.00

The first open ended question that we posed to the participating libraries was: **Please list the five on-line services that accounted for the highest percentage of your library's on-line spending in 1997 and how much you spent on each in that year.** Following is a list of the answers received and a description of the type of academic library that provided the answer.

The library didn't spend any money for commercial on-line services in 1997. "We are part of the University System of Georgia's GALILEO project; we have access to hundreds of on-line journal citations (some full-text) as a member of this project. For this access, we individually, do not pay anything." In 1998 the library plans to spend $850.00 for specific journals not included in GALILEO. - Public, Two-Year School with between 2201 and 3500 students

In 1997, we used Lexis Nexus, OCLC, Psych Abstract, MLA Bibliography, and Newswatch. - Public, Two-Year School with between 3501 and 7750 students

In 1997, we used Chemical Abstracts, FirstSearch, and OCLC. - Public, Four-Year School with more than 7501 students

In 1997, we used reduced price Info Access Product, EbscoHost, and Proquest. - Public, Two-Year School with 7501 students or more

In 1997, we used OCL FirstSearch. - Public, Four-Year School with between 3501 and 7500 students

In 1997, we used FirstSearch, Search Bank, and OCLC. - Public, Two-Year School with between 2201 and 3500 students

In 1997, we used ProQuest, IEC, and FirstSearch. - Private, Four-Year School with between 3501 and 7750 students

In 1997, we used FirstSearch $17,000, IEC $17,000, J Store $2500, Lion $4500, and R-Gender Watch $5000. - Private, Four-Year School with 2200 students or fewer.

In 1997, we used: Oberlin Group, Info Access, Search Bank, Congressional Universe, Academic Universe, and Statistic Universe. - Private, Four-Year School with between 3501 and 7750 students

In 1997, we used OCLC, ProQuest, and FirstSearch. - Private, Four-Year School with 2200 students or fewer

In 1997, we used UALC, OCLC, and RLG. - Private, Four-Year School with 7751 students or more

In 1997, we used Researcher, NewsBank, and NC Live. - Public, Two-Year School with 2200 students or fewer

In 1997, we used only NC Live, No charge. - Public, Two-Year School with between 2201 and 3500 students

In 1997, we used FirstSearch, OCLC. - Private, Four-Year School with 2200 students or fewer

In 1997, we used: IAC, Infotrack, and EbscoHost. - Public, Two-Year School with between 3501 and 7750 students

In 1997, we used: Umi ProQuest, OCLC, and FirstSearch. - Private, Four-Year School with between 2201 and 3500 students

In 1997, we used: EbscoHost, Ethnocrewswatch, Busine, and Psych Lit. - Public, Four-Year School with 7751 students or more

In 1997, we used only Lexis Nexus. - Private, Four-Year School with between 2201 and 3500 students

In 1997, we used Ebscohost, Lexis Nexus, Chem Abstracts, and Dialog. - Private, Four-Year School with between 2201 and 3500 students

In 1997, we used: Information Access, Lexis Nexus, Psych Lit, Social File, and Compact Disclosure. - Private, Four-Year School with between 3501 and 7750 students

In 1997, we only use FirstSearch. - Private, Four-Year School with 2200 students or fewer

In 1997, we use EbscoHost, Eric, and Ginahl. - Private, Four-Year School with between 2201 and 3500 students

In 1997 we use the on-line services Elsevier Academic Press and Academic Universe. - Public, Four-Year School with 7501 students or more

In 1997, $200 was spent on the on-line service KI, and $100 was spent on the on-line service, STN. - Public, Four-Year School with 220 students or fewer

In 1997 the library spent $768.00 on the on-line service STN, $676.00 on the service Dialog, and $508.00 on the service Datatimes. - Private, Four-Year School with between 3501 and 7750 students

In 1997 the library paid for the on-line services, EBSCO, Newsbank, CINAHL, and Baker & Taylor. - Public, Two-Year School with between 2201 and 3500 students

In 1997 the library paid for the on-line services FirstSearch and Dialog @ Carl. - Public, Four-Year School with 7751 students or more

In 1997 the library paid for the on-line service Dialog. - Public, Four-Year School with between 3501 and 7500 students

In 1997 the library paid for the on-line services Engineering Index, MLA International, Sociofile, Applied Science and Technology Index, Aquatic Sciences and Fisheries. - Public, Four-Year School with 7751 students or more

In 1997 the library spent $46,757.00 for the on-line service FirstSearch--OCLC, $21,680.00 on Expanded Academic Index, $21,450.00 on ABI Inform UMI, $5,266.00 on Cambridge Science Abstracts, and $4,170 on Washington Newspapers UMI. - Private, Four-Year School with between 2201 and 3500 students

In 1997 the library spent $3900.00 for OCLC for Interlibrary Loan. - Public, Two-Year School with 7751 students or more

In 1997 the library paid for the on-line service Information Network OFKS. - Public, Four-Year School with between 3501 and 7750 students

In 1997 the library spent $6,255.00 on the on-line service Engineering Index. - Public, Four-Year School with 2200 students or fewer

In 1997 the library spent 100% of its on-line budget on the on-line service UMI. - Public, Two-Year School with 7751 students or more

In 1997 the library paid for the on-line services WLN, EBSCO HOST Academic Elite, and OCLC FirstSearch. - Private, Four-Year School with 2200 students or fewer

In 1997 the library spent $26,000.00 for the on-line service LUIS databases, $19,800.00 on LEXIS/NEXUS, $2,520.00 on Westlaw, and $1,785.00 on Dow Jones. - Public, Four-Year School with 7751 students or more

In 1997 the library paid for the on-line services OCLC, FirstSearch and ProQuest Direct. - Private, Four-Year School with 2200 students or fewer

In 1997 the library spent $9,000.00 for the on-line service UMI-ProQuest, and $8,000.00 for the service InfoTrax. - Public, Two-Year School with between 2201 and 3500 students

In 1997 the library spent $4,000.00 for the on-line service EBSCOhost, $1,000.00 for the service DIALOG, and $650.00 for the service FirstSearch. - Private, Four-Year School with 2200 students or fewer

In 1997 the library spent $12,000.00 for the on-line service InfoTrac and $1,000.00 for the on-line service FirstSearch. - Private, Four-Year School with between 3501 and 7750 students

In 1997 the library spent $10,500.00 on FirstSearch on-line service, $9,000.00 on IAC service, and $1,000.00 on TLC service. - Private, Four-Year School with 2200 students or fewer

In 1997 the library paid for the on-line services DIALOG and OCLC FirstSearch. - Public, Two-year School with 2200 students or fewer

In 1997 the library paid for the on-line services FirstSearch, UMI's ProQuest Direct, and Lexis-Nexus Universe. - Private, Four-Year School with between 2201 and 3500 students

In 1997 the library paid for the on-line services OCLC, BCR, and INLEX. - Private, Two-Year School with 2200 students or fewer

The library spent money on the on-line services, Wilson, DIALOG, and ERIC. - Private, Four-Year School with 2200 students or fewer

In 1997 the library paid for the on-line services J-Store, Ovid, Project Muse, and World News Connection. - Private, Four-Year School with between 2201 and 3500 students

In 1997 the library paid for the on-line services, ProQuest Direct, and Lexis Nexus. - Private, Four-Year School with between 2201 and 3500 students

In 1997 the library paid for the on-line services of South Carolina Discus Program and Britannica Online. - Private, Four-Year School with 2200 students or less

In 1997 the library paid for the online services EBSCO and Library Corporation. - Public, Two-Year School with between 2201 and 3500 students

In 1997 the library paid for the online services AVI Inform Periodical Abstract Online, BIOS, Soc Abstracts, Psychology Info, and Lexis Nexus. - Private, Four-Year School with between 2201 and 3500 students

In 1997 the library paid for the online service VIVA (Galileo). - Public, Four-Year School with between 3501 and 7750 students

In 1997 the library spent $32,000 for the online service FirstSearch, $21,000 for ABI Inform, $16,000 for Lexis Nexis, $20,000 for Chemical Abstracts, and $18,000 for the Academic Expanded Index. - Private, Four-Year School with 7751 students or more

In 1997 the library paid for the on-line services Newsbank, Westlaw, and ProQuest Direct. - Public, Two-Year School with between 3501 and 7750 students

In 1997 the library spent $4500.00 for the on-line service FirstSearch Database. - Public, Two-Year School with 2200 students or fewer

In 1997 the library spent $16,000 for the on-line service IAC, $13,000 for Compendex, and $9,000 for Silver Platter. - Public, Four-Year School with 7751 students or more

In 1997 the library spent $18,000 for the on-line service Lexis-Nexis, $9,300 for the service FirstSearch, $5,000 for Ebscohost Academic Search Elite, $4,368 for Business Abstracts, and $4,929 for MLA Bibliography. - Public, Four-Year School with between 3501 and 7750 students

In 1997 the library paid for the on-line service FirstSearch. - Private, Four-Year School with between 3501 and 7750 students

In 1997 the library paid for the on-line services Omaha World Herald, and Brittanica Online. - Private, Four-Year school with 2200 students or fewer

In 1997 the library paid for the on-line services Business Index, and Health Reference Center Academic. - Public, Two-Year School with 7751 students or more

In 1997 the library paid for the on-line services Lexis-Nexus, ISI, and ERIC. - Private, Four-Year School with between 3501 and 7750 students

In 1997 the library spent $9,289 for the online service OCLC. - Public, Two-Year School with 7751 students or more

In 1997 the library paid for the on-line service Moody's Investors. - Public, Two-Year School with between 3501 and 7750 students

In 1997 the library spent $15,000 for the on-line service ProQuest, and also spent for the on-line services EBSCO HOST, Health Reference Center, Books In Print, and College Source. - Public, Two-Year School with 7751 students or more

In 1997 the library paid for the on-line services Business Index, ERIC, Health Star, MedLine and MLA Bibliography. - Private, Four-Year School with between 3501 and 7750 students

In 1997 the library paid for the on-line services ABI Inform and Compendex. - Public, Four-Year School with 7751 students or more

In 1997 the library paid for the on-line services, OCLC, InfoTrack, and College Catalog. - Public, Two-Year School with between 3501 and 7750 students

In 1997 the library paid for the on-line services UMI Proquest, and Wilson Disks. - Public, Two-Year School with 7751 students or more

In 1997 the library paid for the on-line service EBSCO Host. - Public, Two-Year School with 7751 students or more

In 1997 the library paid for the on-line services UMI, FirstSearch. It also used the services PSAIL and NAPCU, for which they got discount rates. - Private, Four-Year School with between 2201 and 3500 students

In 1997 the library paid for the on-line service EBSCOhost. - Private, Four-Year School iwth 2200 students or fewer

In 1997 the library paid for the on-line services UMI ProQuest, and Encyclopedia Brittanica. - Private, Two-Year School with 7751 students or more

In 1997 the library paid for the on-line services OCLC-FirstSearch, EBSCO, and Lexus-Nexus. - Private, Four-Year School with between 3501 and 7750 students

In 1997, we used Lexis Nexus $8000, Eric $600-$700, Engineering Index. - Private, Four-Year School wth between 3501 and 7750 students

CHAPTER SEVEN: INTERNET USAGE

In general, most academic libraries have not substituted internet searching for usage of commercial on-line services. Only 20% of academic librarians said that they had reduced commercial on-line usage by substituting information obtained for free over the internet for information that they had once paid for through an on-line service. Community colleges and small colleges in general were slightly more apt to have done so, but the association between academic library size and the tendency to substitute internet searching for commercial on-line usage was relatively weak, though positive.

As noted in other sections of this report, the main impact of the internet has been to offer an alternative channel from which to access database producers, who now make a lower percentage of their total sales through on-line brokers.

Once again, the larger libraries are more apt to bypass the brokers than the smaller libraries. Nearly 89% of the larger libraries have done so, while only about 54% of libraries serving colleges with less than 2200 students have done so.

Table #86: Percentage of Academic Libraries that have reduced Commercial On-Line Usage by substituting Information obtained for free over the Internet

	YES	NO
All Libraries	20.2%	79.8%

Table #87: Percentage of Academic Libraries that have reduced Commercial On-Line Usage by substituting Information obtained for free over the Internet, Broken Out by Type of Control of the School, Public or Private

Type of Control	YES	NO
Private	17.9%	82.1%
Public	22.2%	77.8%

Table #88: Percentage of Academic Libraries that have reduced Commercial On-Line Usage by substituting Information obtained for free over the Internet, Broken out by Level of the School, Two-Year or Four-Year

Level of the School	YES	NO
Two-Year	22.6%	77.4%
Four-Year	18.9%	81.1%

Table #89: Percentage of Academic Libraries that have reduced Commercial On-Line Usage by substituting Information obtained for free over the Internet, Broken out by Size of the School

Size of the School	YES	NO
1 - 2200	23.8%	76.2%
2201 - 3500	19.0%	81.1%
3501 - 7750	22.7%	77.3%
7751 and Above	15.0%	85.0%

Table #90: Percentage of Academic Libraries that have used the Internet Access Option offered by Major Commercial Databases through the Internet

	YES	NO
All Libraries	68.7%	31.3%

Table #91: Percentage of Academic Libraries that have used the Internet Access Option offered by Major Commercial Databases through the Internet, Broken out by Type of Control of the School, Public or Private

Type of Control	YES	NO
Public	67.4%	32.6%
Private	70.0%	30.0%

Table #92: Percentage of Academic Libraries that have used the Internet Access Option offered by Major Commercial Databases through the Internet, Broken out by Level of the School, Two-Year or Four-Year

Level of the School	YES	NO
Four-Year	75.0%	25.0%
Two-Year	58.6%	41.4%

Table #93: Percentage of Academic Libraries that have used the Internet Access Option offered by Major Commercial Databases through the Internet, Broken out by Size of the School

Size of the School	YES	NO
1 - 2200	54.5%	45.5%
2201 - 3500	72.7%	27.3%
3501 - 7750	60.0%	40.0%
7751 and Above	88.9%	11.1%

Table #94: Percentage of Academic Libraries have found Information on the Internet, available without a fee, that they once purchased through a Commercial On-Line Service

	Yes	No
All Libraries	30.56%	69.44%

Table 95: Percentage of Academic Libraries that have found Information on the Internet, available without a fee, that they once purchased through a Commercial On-Line Service, Broken out by Type of Control of the School, Public or Private

Type of Control	Yes	No
Public	21.05%	78.95%
Private	41.18%	58.82%

Table #96: Percentage of Academic Libraries that have found Information on the Internet, available without a fee, that they once purchased through a Commercial On-Line Service, Broken out by Level of the School, Two-Year or Four-Year

Level of the School	Yes	No
Two-Year	23.08%	76.92%
Four-Year	34.78%	65.22%

Table #97: Percentage of Academic Libraries that have found Information on the Internet, available without a fee, that they once purchased through a Commercial On-Line Service, Broken out by Size of the School

Size of the School	Yes	No
1-2200	30.43%	69.57%
2201-3500	33.34%	66.67%
3501-7750	33.34%	66.67%
7751 and Above	25.00%	75.00%

CHAPTER EIGHT: CD-ROM

CD-ROM spending by the libraries in the sample rose by only 3.39% in 1998-99, less than the 3.98% rate of spending for all libraries in the sample. Smaller libraries are more apt than larger libraries to maintain high rates of spending on CD-ROM. However, many small libraries appear to be "on the fence" over whether or not to spend less on CD-ROM's and more for on-line accessed databases. It may be that smaller libraries do not have the economies of scale to qualify for consortium programs to obtain the lower database telecom-access prices that many large libraries now enjoy. Or it may be that the ease of use of CD-ROM's have made them favorites with smaller libraries that have less staff to deal with questions about using on-line services, and have less pressing need for the more targeted information often needed for upper level academic research intended for major journals. CD-ROM's show up very often in our requests for "name the best purchase that your library has ever made". They will have a library market for a long time, but they have lost their cachet as "the technology of the future."

CD-ROM's are appreciated, but they are losing out in the price war with on-line services. Interestingly, the mean number of workstations with CD-ROM access that 4-year college libraries would add if CD-ROM vendors were to offer to reduce their prices for multi-workstation licenses by 20% was 3. This suggests a relatively high elasticity of demand for CD-ROM database licenses. However, most vendors that sell their databases on CD-ROM also offer them on-line and may fear cannibalization of their on-line sales.

Table #98: Total Mean Academic Library CD-ROM Spending, 1997-98 and 1998-99 ($ in thousands)

	Mean Spending	Median Spending	Minimum	Maximum
1997-98	11.20	6.00	0.00	54.44
1998-99	11.58	6.00	0.00	60.00

Table #99: Mean Academic Library CD-ROM Spending, Broken out by Type of Control of the School, Public or Private, 1997-98 ($ in thousands)

Type of Control	Mean Spending	Median Spending	Minimum	Maximum
Public	10.67	5.00	0.00	54.44
Private	21.44	8.00	0.00	305.12

Table #100: Mean Academic Library CD-ROM Spending, Broken out by Level of the School, Two-Year or Four-Year, 1997-98 ($ in thousands)

Level of the School	Mean Spending	Median Spending	Minimum	Maximum
Two-Year	6.15	4.60	0.00	20.00
Four-Year	22.86	9.50	0.00	305.16

Table #101: Mean Academic Library CD-ROM Spending, Broken out by Size of the School, 1997-98 ($ in thousands)

Size of the School	Mean Spending	Median Spending	Minimum	Maximum
1-2200	6.50	4.39	0.00	30.00
2201-3500	15.01	7.25	0.00	61.51
3501-7750	13.28	6.85	1.25	51.71
7751 and above	34.24	9.00	1.00	305.16

Table #102: Mean Academic Library CD-ROM Spending, Broken out by Type of Control of the School, Public or Private, 1998-99 ($ in thousands)

Type of Control	Mean Spending	Median Spending	Minimum	Maximum
Public	10.68	4.15	0.00	60.00
Private	12.17	6.85	0.00	50.00

Table #103: Mean Academic Library CD-ROM Spending, Broken out by Level of the School, Two-Year or Four-Year, 1998-99 ($ in thousands)

Level of the School	Mean Spending	Median Spending	Minimum	Maximum
Two-Year	5.93	3.50	0.00	25.00
Four-Year	15.27	8.75	0.00	60.00

Table #104: Mean Academic Library CD-ROM Spending, Broken out by Size of the School, 1998-99 ($ in thousands)

Size of the School	Mean Spending	Median Spending	Minimum	Maximum
1-2200	6.04	4.39	0.00	20.00
2201-3500	14.31	6.88	0.00	50.00
3501-7750	13.68	12.00	0.00	60.00
7751 and above	14.06	7.88	0.00	60.00

Table #105: Total Mean Number of CD-ROM Database Subscriptions Maintained by Academic Libraries

	Mean Number	Median Number	Minimum	Maximum
All Libraries	7	4	0	60

Table #106: Mean Number of CD-ROM Database Subscriptions Maintained by Academic Libraries, Broken out by Type of Control of the School, Public or Private

Type of Control	Mean Number	Median Number	Minimum	Maximum
Public	6	4	0	29
Private	9	6	0	60

Table #107: Mean Number of CD-ROM Database Subscriptions Maintained by Academic Libraries, Broken out by Level of the School, Two-Year or Four-Year

Level of the School	Mean Number	Median Number	Minimum	Maximum
Two-Year	4	3	0	20
Four-Year	9	6	0	60

Table #108: Mean Number of CD-ROM Database Subscriptions Maintained by Academic Libraries, Broken out by Size of the School

Size of the School	Mean Number	Median Number	Minimum	Maximum
1-2200	4	4	0	16
2201-3500	7	5	0	40
3501-7750	8	6	1	23
7751 and Above	12	7	0	60

Table #109: Percentage of Academic Libraries that Plan to Increase, Decrease, and Maintain the Same Number of CD-ROM Databases in the next Two Years

	Increase	Stay the Same	Decrease
All Libraries	17.14%	57.14%	25.71%

Table #110: Percentage of Academic Libraries that Plan to Increase, Decrease, and Maintain the Same Number of CD-ROM Databases in the next Two Years, Broken out by Type of Control of the School, Public or Private

Type of Control	Increase	Stay the Same	Decrease
Public	17.14%	54.29%	28.57%
Private	17.14%	60.00%	22.86%

Table #111: Percentage of Academic Libraries that Plan to Increase, Decrease, and Maintain the Same Number of CD-ROM Databases in the next Two Years, Broken out by Level of the School, Two-Year or Four-Year

Level of the School	Increase	Stay the Same	Decrease
Two-Year	19.23%	50.00%	30.77%
Four-Year	15.91%	61.36%	22.73%

Table #112: Percentage of Academic Libraries that Plan to Increase, Decrease, and Maintain the Same Number of CD-ROM Databases in the next Two Years, Broken out by Size of the School

Size of the School	Increase	Stay the Same	Decrease
1-2200	9.52%	71.43%	19.05%
2201-3500	27.78%	55.56%	16.67%
3501-7750	12.50%	43.75%	43.75%
7751 and Above	20.00%	53.34%	26.67%

*Numbers may not add up to 100.00 due to rounding

Table #113: Mean Number of Workstations Academic Libraries would add to a CD-ROM License if Database Vendors were willing to decrease their Price by 20%

	Mean Number	Median Number	Minimum	Maximum
All Libraries	2	1	0	24

Table #114: Mean Number of Workstations Academic Libraries would add to a CD-ROM License if Database Vendors were willing to decrease their Price by 20%, Broken out by Type of Control of the School, Public or Private

Type of Control	Mean Number	Median Number	Minimum	Maximum
Public	1	0	0	8
Private	2	1	0	24

Table #115: Mean Number of Workstations Academic Libraries would add to a CD-ROM License if Database Vendors were willing to decrease their Price by 20%, Broken out by Level of the School, Two-Year or Four-Year

Level of the School	Mean Number	Median Number	Minimum	Maximum
Two-Year	1	1	0	8
Four-Year	3	1	0	24

Table #116: Mean Number of Workstations Academic Libraries would add to a CD-ROM License if Database Vendors were willing to decrease their Price by 20%, Broken out by Size of the School

Size of the School	Mean Number	Median Number	Minimum	Maximum
1-2200	3	1	0	23
2201-3500	1	1	0	6
3501-7750	2	2	0	8
7751 and Above	3	0	0	24

Table #117: Total Mean Number of CD-ROM Subscriptions that Academic Libraries Added or Planned to Add, 1997-98 and 1998-99

	Mean Number	Median Number	Minimum	Maximum	Percent Mean Increase
1997-98	1	0	0	15	
1998-99	1	0	0	12	0.00%

Table #118: Mean Number of CD-ROM Subscriptions Added by Academic Libraries, Broken out by Type of Control of the School, Public or Private, 1997-98

Type of Control	Mean Number	Median Number	Minimum	Maximum
Public	1	0	0	4
Private	1	0	0	15

Table #119: Mean Number of CD-ROM Subscriptions Added by Academic Libraries, Broken out by Level of the School, Two-Year or Four-Year, 1997-98

Level of the School	Mean Number	Median Number	Minimum	Maximum
Two-Year	1	0	0	5
Four-Year	1	0	0	15

Table #120: Mean Number of CD-ROM Subscriptions Added by Academic Libraries, Broken out by Size of the School, 1997-98

Size of the School	Mean Number	Median Number	Minimum	Maximum
1-2200	1	0	0	15
2201-3500	1	0	0	4
3501-7750	1	0	0	4
7751 and Above	1	0	0	6

Table #121: Mean Number of CD-ROM Subscriptions that Academic Libraries Plan to Add in 1998-99, Broken out by Type of Control of the School, Public or Private

Type of Control	Mean Number	Median Number	Minimum	Maximum
Public	1	0	0	9
Private	1	0	0	12

Table #122: Mean Number of CD-ROM Subscriptions that Academic Libraries Plan to Add in 1998-99, Broken out by Level of the School, Two-Year or Four-Year

Level of the School	Mean Number	Median Number	Minimum	Maximum
Two-Year	1	0	0	9
Four-Year	1	0	0	12

Table #123: Mean Number of CD-ROM Subscriptions that Academic Libraries Plan to Add in 1998-99, Broken out by Size of the School

Size of the School	Mean Number	Median Number	Minimum	Maximum
1-2200	1	0	0	12
2201-3500	0	0	0	3
3501-7750	0	0	0	5
7751 and Above	2	1	0	9

Table #124: Total Mean Number of CD-ROM Database Subscriptions that Academic Libraries Dropped or Planned to Drop, 1997-98 and 1998-99

	Mean Number	Median Number	Minimum	Maximum
1997-98	1	0	0	13
1998-99	1	0	0	5

Table #125: Mean Number of CD-ROM Database Subscriptions Added by Academic Libraries in 1997-98, Broken out by Type of Control of the School, Public or Private

Type of Control	Mean Number	Median Number	Minimum	Maximum
Public	1	0	0	6
Private	1	0	0	13

Table #126: Mean Number of CD-ROM Database Subscriptions Added by Academic Libraries in 1997-98, Broken out by Level of the School, Two-Year or Four-Year

Level of the School	Mean Number	Median Number	Minimum	Maximum
Two-Year	1	0	0	3
Four-Year	1	0	0	13

Table #127: Mean Number of CD-ROM Database Subscriptions Added by Academic Libraries in 1997-98, Broken out by Size of the School

Size of the School	Mean Number	Median Number	Minimum	Maximum
1-2200	1	0	0	3
2201-3500	1	0	0	8
3501-7750	1	0	0	6
7751 and Above	3	2	0	13

Table #128: Mean Number of CD-ROM Database Subscriptions that Academic Libraries Plan to Add in 1998-99, Broken out by Type of Control of the School, Public or Private

Type of Control	Mean Number	Median Number	Minimum	Maximum
Public	1	0	0	5
Private	1	0	0	5

Table #129: Mean Number of CD-ROM Database Subscriptions that Academic Libraries Plan to Add in 1998-99, Broken out by Level of the School, Two-Year or Four-Year

Level of the School	Mean Number	Median Number	Minimum	Maximum
Two-Year	1	0	0	5
Four-Year	1	1	0	5

Table #130: Mean Number of CD-ROM Database Subscriptions that Academic Libraries Plan to Add in 1998-99, Broken out by Size of the School

Size of the School	Mean Number	Median Number	Minimum	Maximum
1-2200	1	0	0	4
2201-3500	1	0	0	5
3501-7750	1	0	0	5
7751 and Above	2	2	0	5

Table #131: Percent of Academic Libraries that have a DVD Player

	YES	NO
All Libraries	8.60%	91.4%

Table #132: Percent of Libraries that have a DVD Player, Broken out by Type of Control of the School, Public or Private

Type of Control	YES	NO
Public	6.52%	93.5%
Private	10.9%	89.1%

Table #133: Percent of Libraries that have a DVD Player, Broken out by Level of the School, Two-Year or Four-Year

Level of the School	YES	NO
Four-Year	7.02%	93.1%
Two-Year	11.8%	88.2%

Table #134: Percent of Libraries that have a DVD Player, Broken out by Size of the School

Size of the School	YES	NO
1 - 2200	8.33%	91.7%
2201 - 3500	8.33%	91.7%
3501 - 7750	9.10%	90.9%
7751 and Above	9.10%	90.9%

Table #135: Percent of Libraries that Plan to Purchase a DVD Player Next Year

	YES	NO
All Libraries	16.5%	83.5%

Table #136: Percent of Libraries that Plan to Purchase a DVD Player Next Year, Broken out by Type of Control of the School, Public or Private

Type of Control	YES	NO
Private	12.8%	87.2%
Public	20.0%	80.0%

Table #137: Percent of Libraries that Plan to Purchase a DVD Player Next Year, Broken out by Level of the College, Two-Year or Four-Year

Level of the School	YES	NO
Four-Year	9.80%	90.2%
Two-Year	27.3%	72.7%

Table #138: Percent of Libraries that Plan to Purchase a DVD Player Next Year, Broken out by Size of the School.

Size of the School	YES	NO
1 - 2200	0.0%	100.0%
2201 - 3500	20.8%	79.2%
3501 - 7750	25.0%	75.0%
7751 and Above	20.0%	80.0%

Table #139: Total Mean Number of CD-ROM Readers Maintained by Academic Libraries

	Mean Number	Median Number	Minimum	Maximum
All Libraries	24	10	0	300

Table #140: Mean Number of CD-ROM Readers Maintained by Academic Libraries, Broken out by Type of Control of the School, Public or Private

Type of Control	Mean Number	Median Number	Minimum	Maximum
Public	28	9	0	300
Private	19	13	0	200

Table #141: Mean Number of CD-ROM Readers Maintained by Academic Libraries, Broken out by Level of the School, Two-Year or Four-Year

Level of the School	Mean Number	Median Number	Minimum	Maximum
Two-Year	14	7	0	160
Four-Year	30	14	0	300

Table #142: Mean Number of CD-ROM Readers Maintained by Academic Libraries, Broken out by Size of the School

Size of the School	Mean Number	Median Number	Minimum	Maximum
1-2200	10	7	0	31
2201-3500	17	10	1	160
3501-7750	16	10	0	60
7750 and Above	52	23	5	300

CHAPTER NINE: AUDIO-VIDEO

Spending for audio materials such as audio cd's and cassettes rose by 5.89% in 1998, spurred by increases in spending on audio books. It will be interesting to see how the spread of interactive voice technology into the information services industry will affect academic libraries. We did not include any questions to this effect in the survey, since the technology has not yet been seriously introduced into the information services industry. However, it soon will be. Voice recognition technology is fast improving and, within 5 years, many scholars may be composing their works through voice recognition software that recognizes words and translates them into computer text that can be easily manipulated. Voice recognition technology may very well be the means to translate difficult to use computing devices into easy to use appliances.

In libraries, voice recognition technology will have many highly beneficial applications. The use of voice to catalog books and periodicals, to record scholarly research notes, even to access the internet without the innumerable and ponderous clicks and long waits now necessary -- are all real possibilities over the next five years.

Our feeling is that library trade associations should be monitoring the progress of voice recognition technology and develop ties with leading trade associations of voice equipment and technology manufacturers. Both parties should be exploring possible applications.

Video materials spending rose by 12.67% but the number of libraries responding to the question was only 44.

Table #143: Total Mean Academic Library Audio Materials Spending, 1997-98 and 1998-99 ($ in thousands)

	Mean Spending	Median Spending	Minimum	Maximum	Percent Mean Increase
1997-98	4.75	0.25	0.00	56.00	
1998-99	5.03	0.20	0.00	56.00	5.89

Table #144: Mean Academic Library Audio Materials Spending, Broken out by Type of Control of the School, Public or Private, 1997-98 ($ in thousands)

Type of Control	Mean Spending	Median Spending	Minimum	Maximum
Public	2.83	0.06	0.00	50.00
Private	8.09	1.00	0.00	56.00

Table #145: Mean Academic Library Audio Materials Spending, Broken out by Level of the School, Two-Year or Four-Year, 1997-98 ($ in thousands)

Level of the School	Mean Spending	Median Spending	Minimum	Maximum
Two-Year	0.90	0.11	0.00	4.20
Four-Year	7.40	0.50	0.00	56.00

Table #146: Mean Academic Library Audio Materials Spending, Broken out by Size of the School, 1997-98 ($ in thousands)

Size of School	Mean Spending	Median Spending	Minimum	Maximum
1-2200	2.11	0.20	0.00	20.00
2201-3500	5.34	0.50	0.00	42.00
3501-7750	1.70	0.25	0.00	9.00
7751 and Above	9.90	1.35	0.00	56.00

Table #147: Mean Academic Library Audio Materials Spending, Broken out by Type of Control of the School, Public or Private, 1998-99 ($ in thousands)

Type of Control	Mean Spending	Median Spending	Minimum	Maximum
Public	3.12	0.00	0.00	50.00
Private	7.84	1.50	0.00	56.00

Table #148: Mean Academic Library Audio Materials Spending, Broken out by Level of the School, Two-Year or Four-Year, 1998-99 ($ in thousands)

Level of the School	Mean Spending	Median Spending	Minimum	Maximum
Two-Year	0.76	0.01	0.00	5.00
Four-Year	7.37	0.50	0.00	56.00

Table #149: Mean Academic Library Audio Materials Spending, Broken out by Size of the School, 1998-99 ($ in thousands)

Size of the School	Mean Spending	Median Spending	Minimum	Maximum
1-2200	2.95	0.20	0.00	25.00
2201-3500	3.45	0.36	0.00	35.00
3501-7750	1.47	0.00	0.00	9.27
7751 and Above	13.50	1.50	0.00	56.00

Table #150: Mean Academic Library Audio Materials Spending, 1996-97 ($ in thousands)

	Mean Spending	Median Spending	Minimum	Maximum
All Libraries	3.97	0.20	0.00	56.00

Table #151: Mean Academic Library Audio Materials Spending, Broken out by Type of Control of the School, Public or Private, 1996-97 ($ in thousands)

Type of Control	Mean Spending	Median Spending	Minimum	Maximum
Public	2.49	0.00	0.00	50.00
Private	5.66	0.50	0.00	56.00

Table #152: Mean Academic Library Audio Materials Spending, Broken out by Level of the School, Two-Year or Four-Year, 1996-97 ($ in thousands)

Level of the School	Mean Spending	Median Spending	Minimum	Maximum
Public	0.49	0.01	0.00	4.00
Private	5.55	0.50	0.00	56.00

Table #153: Mean Academic Library Audio Materials Spending, Broken out by Size of the School, 1996-97 ($ in thousands)

Size of the School	Mean Spending	Median Spending	Minimum	Maximum
1-2200	0.64	0.13	0.00	4.50
2201-3500	3.76	0.26	0.00	35.30
3501-7750	1.34	0.00	0.00	8.35
7751 and Above	11.41	1.15	0.00	56.00

Table #154: Total Mean Academic Library Video Materials Spending, 1997-98 and 1998-99 ($ in thousands)

	Mean Spending	Median Spending	Minimum	Maximum	Percent Mean Increase
1997-98	8.13	4.00	0.00	50.00	
1998-99	9.16	5.00	0.00	50.00	12.67

Table #155: Mean Academic Library Video Materials Spending, Broken out by Type of Control of the School, Public or Private, 1997-98 ($ in thousands)

Type of Control	Mean Spending	Median Spending	Minimum	Maximum
Public	8.17	6.00	0.00	50.00
Private	9.48	3.00	0.00	50.00

Table #156: Mean Academic Library Video Materials Spending, Broken out by Level of the School, Two-Year or Four-Year, 1997-98 ($ in thousands)

Level of the School	Mean Spending	Median Spending	Minimum	Maximum
Two-Year	8.43	8.00	0.00	25.00
Four-Year	8.93	2.00	0.00	50.00

Table #157: Mean Academic Library Video Materials Spending, Broken out by Size of the School, 1997-98 ($ in thousands)

Size of the School	Mean Spending	Median Spending	Minimum	Maximum
1-2200	5.50	3.00	0.00	25.00
2201-3500	9.92	9.00	0.00	25.00
3501-7750	4.14	1.50	0.00	15.00
7751 and Above	14.66	10.00	0.00	50.00

Table #158: Mean Academic Library Video Materials Spending, Broken out by Type of Control of the School, Public or Private, 1998-99 ($ in thousands)

Type of Control	Mean Spending	Median Spending	Minimum	Maximum
Public	7.73	5.00	0.00	50.00
Private	11.96	5.50	0.00	50.00

Table #159: Mean Academic Library Video Materials Spending, Broken out by Level of the School, Two-Year or Four-Year, 1998-99 ($ in thousands)

Level of the School	Mean Spending	Median Spending	Minimum	Maximum
Two-Year	6.13	5.00	0.00	15.00
Four-Year	11.48	5.00	0.00	50.00

Table #160: Mean Academic Library Video Materials Spending, Broken out by Size of the School, 1998-99 ($ in thousands)

Size of the School	Mean Spending	Median Spending	Minimum	Maximum
1-2200	8.76	5.00	0.00	50.00
2201-3500	10.22	12.00	0.00	31.00
3501-7750	1.83	0.50	0.00	8.00
7751 and Above	15.26	7.50	0.00	50.00

Table #161: Total Mean Academic Library Video Materials Spending, 1996-97 ($ in thousands)

	Mean Spending	Median Spending	Minimum	Maximum
All Libraries	6.83	2.50	0.00	50.00

Table #162: Total Mean Academic Library Video Materials Spending, Broken out by Type of Control of the School, Public or Private, 1996-97 ($ in thousands)

Type of Control	Mean Spending	Median Spending	Minimum	Maximum
Public	6.08	4.00	0.00	50.00
Private	7.81	1.50	0.00	50.00

Table #163: Total Mean Academic Library Video Materials Spending, Broken out by Level of the School, Two-Year or Four-Year, 1996-97 ($ in thousands)

Level of the School	Mean Spending	Median Spending	Minimum	Maximum
Two-Year	5.31	4.40	0.00	15.00
Four-Year	7.69	1.15	0.00	50.00

Table #164: Total Mean Academic Library Video Materials Spending, Broken out by Size of the School, 1996-97 ($ in thousands)

Size of the School	Mean Spending	Median Spending	Minimum	Maximum
1-2200	4.56	2.00	0.00	25.00
2201-3500	6.64	5.00	0.00	17.00
3501-7750	1.16	0.00	0.00	5.00
7751 and Above	14.08	3.25	0.00	50.00

CHAPTER TEN: CATALOGING

Table #165: Percentage of Libraries whose Catalogs are available On-Line (Internal Network)

	YES	NO
All Libraries	88.8%	11.2%

Table #166: Percentage of Libraries whose Catalogs are available On-Line (Internal Network), Broken out by Type of Control of the School, Public or Private

Type of Control	YES	NO
Public	90.2%	9.80%
Private	89.4%	10.6%

Table #167: Percentage of Libraries whose Catalogs are available On-Line (Internal Network), Broken out by Level of the School, Two-Year or Four-Year

Level of the School	YES	NO
Two-Year	88.9%	11.1%
Four-Year	90.3%	9.68%

Table #168: Percentage of Libraries whose Catalogs are available On-Line (Internal Network), Broken out by Size of the School

Size of the School	YES	NO
1 - 2200	88.5%	11.5%
2201 - 3500	84.6%	15.4%
3501 - 7750	95.5%	4.55%
7751 and Above	91.7%	8.33%

Table #169: Percentage of Libraries whose Catalogs are available in CD-ROM Form

	YES	NO
All Libraries	14.4%	85.6%

Table #170: Percentage of Libraries whose Catalogs are available in CD-ROM Form, Broken out by Type of Control of the School, Public or Private

Type of Control	YES	NO
Public	9.80%	90.2%
Private	19.6%	80.4%

Table #171: Percentage of Libraries whose Catalogs are available in CD-ROM Form, Broken out by Level of the College, Two-Year or Four-Year

Level of the School	YES	NO
Two-Year	8.33%	91.7%
Four-Year	18.0%	82.0%

Table #172: Percentage of Libraries whose Catalogs are available in CD-ROM Form, Broken out by Size of School

Size of the School	YES	NO
1 - 2200	8.0%	92.0%
2201 - 3500	32.0%	68.0%
3501 - 7750	0.0%	100.0%
7751 and Above	16.7%	83.3%

Table #173: Percentage of Libraries whose Catalogs are available in the Paper Card Catalog

	YES	NO
All Libraries	16.3%	83.7%

Table #174: Percentage of Libraries whose Catalogs are available in the Paper Card Catalog, Broken out by Type of Control of the School, Public or Private

Type of Control	YES	NO
Public	15.4%	84.6%
Private	15.2%	84.8%

Table #175: Percentage of Libraries whose Catalogs are available in the Paper Card Catalog, Broken out by Level of the College, Two-Year or Four-Year

Level of the School	YES	NO
Two-Year	16.2%	83.8%
Four-Year	14.8%	85.2%

Table #176: Percentage of Libraries whose Catalogs are available in the Paper Card Catalog, Broken out by Size of the School

Size of the School	YES	NO
1 - 2200	30.8%	69.2%
2201 - 3500	4.0%	96.0%
3501 - 7750	13.0%	87.0%
7751 and Above	12.5%	87.5%

Table #177: Percentage of Libraries whose Catalogs are available on the Internet or World Wide Web

	Yes	No
All Libraries	72.73%	27.27%

Table #178: Percentage of Libraries whose Catalogs are available on the Internet or World Wide Web, Broken out by Type of Control of the School, Public or Private

Type of Control	Yes	No
Public	69.23%	30.77%
Private	76.60%	23.40%

Table #179: Percentage of Libraries whose Catalogs are available on the Internet or World Wide Web, Broken out by Level of the School, Two-Year or Four-Year

Level of the School	Yes	No
Two-Year	56.76%	43.24%
Four-Year	82.26%	17.74%

Table #180: Percentage of Libraries whose Catalogs are available on the Internet or World Wide Web, Broken out by Size of the School

Size of the School	Yes	No
1-2200	61.54%	38.46%
2201-3500	69.23%	30.77%
3501-7750	78.26%	21.74%
7750 and Above	83.34%	16.67%

* Note: Numbers may not add up to 100.00 due to rounding

Table #180: Mean Number of Workstations that offer Access to Academic Libraries' Catalogs

	Mean Number	Median Number	Minimum	Maximum
All Libraries	41	16	0	350

Table #181: Mean Number of Workstations that offer Access to Academic Libraries' Catalogs, Broken out by Type of Control of the School, Public or Private

Type of Control	Mean Number	Median Number	Minimum	Maximum
Public	44	16	0	300
Private	39	20	0	350

Table #182: Mean Number of Workstations that offer Access to Academic Libraries' Catalogs, Broken out by Level of the School, Two-Year or Four-Year

Level of the School	Mean Number	Median Number	Minimum	Maximum
Two-Year	26	13	160	6
Four-Year	51	24	350	10

Table #183: Mean Number of Workstations that offer Access to Academic Libraries' Catalogs, Broken out by Size of the School

Size of the School	Mean Number	Median Number	Minimum	Maximum
1-2200	10	8	0	42
2201-3500	28	14	0	160
3501-7750	36	22	0	150
7751 and Above	92	52	0	350

Table #184: Percentage of Academic Libraries whose Catalogs can be accessed from Outside the Library

	Yes	No
All Libraries	88.04%	11.96%

Table #185: Percentage of Academic Libraries whose Catalogs can be accessed from Outside the Library, Broken out by Type of Control of the School, Public or Private

Type of Control	Yes	No
Public	86.00%	14.00%
Private	90.48%	9.52%

Table #186: Percentage of Academic Libraries whose Catalogs can be accessed from Outside the Library, Broken out by Level of the School, Two-Year or Four-Year

Level of the School	Yes	No
Public	80.00%	20.00%
Private	92.98%	7.02%

Table #187: Percentage of Academic Libraries whose Catalogs can be accessed from Outside the Library, Broken out by Size of the School

Size of the School	Yes	No
1-2200	65.22%	34.78%
2201-3500	92.00%	8.00%
3501-7750	100.00%	0.00%
7751 and Above	95.83%	4.17%

Table #188: Percentage of Libraries Planning to Purchase A New Cataloging System within the next Year

	YES	NO
All Libraries	17.9%	82.1%

Table #189: Percentage of Libraries Planning to Purchase A New Cataloging System within the next Year, Broken out by Type of Control of the School, Public or Private

Type of Control	YES	NO
Private	13.0%	87.1%
Public	22.9%	77.1%

Table #190: Percentage of Libraries Planning to Purchase A New Cataloging System within the next Year, Broken out by Level of the School, Two-Year or Four-Year

Level of the School	YES	NO
Two-Year	17.1%	82.9%
Four-Year	18.3%	81.7%

Table #191: Percentage of Libraries Planning to Purchase A New Cataloging System within the next Year, Broken out by Size of the School

Size of the School	YES	NO
1 - 2200	19.2%	80.8%
2201 - 3500	13.0%	87.0%
3501 - 7750	18.2%	81.8%
7751 and Above	20.8%	79.2%

Table #192: Percentage of Libraries Planning to Purchase a New Cataloging System within the next Three Years

	YES	NO	MAYBE
All Libraries	41.2%	57.6%	1.18%

Table #193: Percentage of Libraries Planning to Purchase a New Cataloging System within the next Three Years, Broken out by Type of Control of the School, Public or Private

Type of Control	YES	NO	MAYBE
Private	35.9%	64.1%	0.00%
Public	46.7%	51.1%	2.22%

Table #194: Percentage of Libraries Planning to Purchase a New Cataloging System within the next Three Years, Broken out by Level of the School, Two-Year or Four-Year

Level of the School	YES	NO	MAYBE
Two-Year	37.5%	62.5%	0.00%
Four-Year	43.4%	54.7%	1.89%

Table #195: Percentage of Libraries Planning to Purchase a New Cataloging System within the next Three Years, Broken out by Size of the School

Size of the School	YES	NO	MAYBE
1 - 2200	45.0%	55.0%	0.00%
2201 - 3500	33.3%	66.7%	0.00%
3501 - 7750	42.9%	57.1%	0.00%
7751 and Above	43.5%	52.2%	4.35%

Table #196: Percentage of Libraries that Outsource Cataloging

	YES	NO
All Libraries	13.3%	86.7%

Table #197: Percentage of Libraries that Outsource Cataloging, Broken out by Type of Control of the School, Public or Private

Type of Control	YES	NO
Private	7.50%	92.5%
Public	18.4%	81.6%

Table #198: Percentage of Libraries that Outsource Cataloging, Broken out by Level of the School, Two-Year or Four-Year

Level of the School	YES	NO
Two-Year	17.6%	82.4%
Four-Year	10.7%	89.3%

Table #199: Percentage of Libraries that Outsource Cataloging, Broken out by Size of School

Size of the School	YES	NO
1 - 2200	17.4%	82.6%
2201 - 3500	9.10%	90.9%
3501 - 7750	9.52%	90.5%
7751 and Above	16.7%	83.3%

Table #200: Percentage of Libraries that Outsource Authority Control

	YES	NO
All Libraries	16.1%	83.9%

Table #201: Percentage of Libraries that Outsource Authority Control, Broken out by Type of Control of the School, Public or Private

Type of Control	YES	NO
Private	16.2%	83.8%
Public	16.3%	83.7%

Table #202: Percentage of Libraries that Outsource Authority Control, Broken out by Level of the School, Two-Year or Four-Year

Level of the School	YES	NO
Two-Year	11.8%	88.2%
Four-Year	18.9%	81.1%

Table #203: Percentage of Libraries that Outsource Authority Control, Broken out by Size of the School

Size of the School	YES	NO
1 - 2200	4.35%	95.7%
2201 - 3500	25.0%	75.0%
3501 - 7750	14.3%	85.7%
7751 and Above	21.7%	78.3%

CHAPTER TEN: LIBRARY SOFTWARE

More than 85% of the libraries in the sample reported that they use a form of integrated library software. Roughly 70% of libraries serving colleges with student populations of less than 2200 had integrated library software packages, while 95% of libraries serving colleges with more than 7500 students had such packages. Size of the school served by the library and propensity to use an integrated library software system were closely related,though high percentages of libraries in any size range use an integrated library system. Most systems generated management statistical reports.

Cataloging and on-line catalog access were almost always controlled by the integrated library system, while book acquisitions and serials control were often controlled by the integrated library software system. Media purchases and management were under the purview of the integrated library system in about one half of cases.

Table #204: Percentage of Libraries that have an Integrated Library Software System

	YES	NO
All Libraries	85.1%	14.9%

Table #205: Percentage of Libraries that have an Integrated Library Software System, Broken out by Type of Control of the School, Public or Private

Type of Control	YES	NO
Private	88.6%	11.4%
Public	83.7%	16.3%

Table #206: Percentage of Libraries that have an Integrated Library Software System, Broken out by Level of the School, Two-Year or Four-Year

Level of the School	YES	NO
Two-Year	82.9%	17.1%
Four-Year	86.4%	13.6%

Table #207: Percentage of Libraries that have an Integrated Library Software System, Broken out by Size of the School

Size of the School	YES	NO
1 - 2200	70.8%	29.2%
2201 - 3500	84.0%	16.0%
3501 - 7750	90.9%	9.10%
7751 and Above	95.7%	4.35%

Table #208: Percentage of Libraries for whom Cataloging is a Function of the Integrated Software System

	YES	NO
All Libraries	96.3%	3.66%

Table #209: Percentage of Libraries for whom Cataloging is a Function of the Integrated Software System, Broken out by Type of Control of the School, Public or Private

Type of Control	YES	NO
Private	97.5%	2.50%
Public	95.2%	4.80%

Table #210: Percentage of Libraries for whom Cataloging is a Function of the Integrated Software System, Broken out by Level of the School, Two-Year or Four-Year

Level of the School	YES	NO
Two-Year	96.7%	3.33%
Four-Year	96.2%	3.85%

Table #211: Percentage of Libraries for whom Cataloging is a Function of the Integrated Software System, Broken out by Size of the School

Size of the School	YES	NO
1 - 2200	94.4%	5.6%
2201 - 3500	100.0%	0.0%
3501 - 7750	100.0%	0.0%
7751 and Above	91.3%	8.7%

Table #212: Percentage of Libraries for whom On-Line Public Access is Controlled by the Integrated Software System

	YES	NO
All Libraries	88.8%	11.3%

Table #213: Percentage of Libraries for whom On-Line Public Access is Controlled by the Integrated Software System, Broken out by Type of Control of the School, Public or Private

Type of Control	YES	NO
Private	92.1%	7.90%
Public	85.7%	12.2%

Table #214: Percentage of Libraries for whom On-Line Public Access in Controlled by the Integrated Software System, Broken out by Level of the School, Two-Year or Four-Year

Level of the School	YES	NO
Two-Year	86.7%	13.3%
Four-Year	90.0%	10.0%

Table #215: Percentage of Libraries for whom On-Line Public Access is Controlled by the Integrated Software System, Broken out by Size of the School

Size of the School	YES	NO
1 - 2200	100.0%	0.0%
2201 - 3500	80.0%	20.0%
3501 - 7750	84.2%	15.9%
7751 and Above	92.2%	8.7%

Table #216: Percentage of Libraries for whom Circulation Control is a Function of the Integrated Software System

	YES	NO
All Libraries	96.3%	3.66%

Table #217: Percentage of Libraries for whom Circulation Control is a Function of the Integrated Software System, Broken out by Type of Control of the School, Public or Private

Type of Control	YES	NO
Private	95.0%	5.00%
Public	97.6%	2.40%

Table #218: Percentage of Libraries for whom Circulation Control is a Function of the Integrated Software System, Broken out by Level of the School, Two-Year or Four-Year

Level of the School	YES	NO
Two-Year	96.7%	3.33%
Four-Year	96.2%	3.85%

Table #219: Percentage of Libraries for whom Circulation Control is a Function of the Integrated Software System, Broken out by Size of the School

Size of the School	YES	NO
1 - 2200	88.9%	11.1
2201 - 3500	95.2%	4.8%
3501 - 7750	100.0%	0.0%
7751 and Above	100.0%	0.0%

Table #220: Percentage of Libraries for whom Acquisitions Control is a Function of the Integrated Software System

	YES	NO
All Libraries	68.3%	28.4%

Table #221: Percentage of Libraries for whom Acquisitions Control is a Function of the Integrated Software System, Broken out by Type of Control of the School, Public or Private

Type of Control	YES	NO
Private	75.0%	25.0%
Public	61.9%	38.1%

Table #222: Percentage of Libraries for whom Acquisitions Control is a Function of the Integrated Software System, Broken out by Level of the School, Two-Year or Four-Year

Level of the School	YES	NO
Two-Year	50.0%	50.0%
Four-Year	78.8%	21.2%

Table #223: Percentage of Libraries for whom Acquisitions Control is a Function of the Integrated Software System, Broken out by Size of the School

Size of the School	YES	NO
1 - 2200	61.1%	38.9%
2201 - 3500	57.1%	42.9%
3501 - 7750	70.0%	30.0%
7751 and Above	82.6%	17.4%

Table #224: Percentage of Libraries for whom Serial Control is a Function of the Integrated Software System

	YES	NO
All Libraries	71.6%	28.4%

Table #225: Percentage of Libraries for whom Serial Control is a Function of the Integrated Software System, Broken out by Type of Control of the School, Public or Private

Type of Control	YES	NO
Private	76.9%	23.1%
Public	66.7%	33.3%

Table #226: Percentage of Libraries for whom Serial Control is a Function of the Integrated Software System, Broken out by Level of the School, Two-Year of Four-Year

Level of the School	YES	NO
Two-Year	56.7%	43.3%
Four-Year	80.4%	19.6%

Table #227: Percentage of Libraries for whom Serial Control is a Function of the Integrated Software System, Broken out by Size of the School

Size of the School	YES	NO
1 - 2200	66.7%	33.3%
2201 - 3500	61.9%	38.1%
3501 - 7750	78.9%	21.1%
7751 and Above	78.3%	21.7%

Table #228: Percentage of Libraries for whom Media Control is a Function of the Integrated Software System

	YES	NO
All Libraries	48.7%	51.3%

Table #229: Percentage of Libraries for whom Media Control is a Function of the Integrated Software System, Broken out by Type of Control of the School, Public or Private

Type of Control	YES	NO
Private	43.2%	56.8%
Public	53.8%	46.2%

Table #230: Percentage of Libraries for whom Media Control is a Function of the Integrated Software System, Broken out by Level of the School, Two-Year or Four-Year

Level of the School	YES	NO
Two-Year	60.7%	39.3%
Four-Year	41.7%	58.3%

Table #231: Percentage of Libraries for whom Media Control is a Function of the Integrated Software System, Broken out by Size of the School

Size of the School	YES	NO
1 - 2200	29.4%	70.6%
2201 - 3500	47.6%	52.4%
3501 - 7750	64.7%	35.3%
7751 and Above	52.4%	47.6%

Table #232: Percentage of Libraries for whom Management Statistical Reports are a Function of the Integrated Software System

	YES	NO
All Libraries	76.5%	23.5%

Table #233: Percentage of Libraries for whom Management Statistical Reports are a Function of the Integrated Software System, Broken out by Type of Control of the School, Public or Private

Type of Control	YES	NO
Private	82.5%	17.5%
Public	70.7%	29.3%

Table #234: Percentage of Libraries for whom Management Statistical Reports are a Function of the Integrated Software System, Broken out by Level of the School, Two-Year or Four-Year

Level of the School	YES	NO
Four-Year	76.5%	23.5%
Two-Year	75.9%	24.1%

Table #235: Percentage of Academic Libraries for whom Management Statistical Reports are a Function of the Integrated Software System, Broken out by Size of the School

Size of the School	YES	NO
1 - 2200	70.6%	29.4%
2201 - 3500	71.4%	28.6%
3501 - 7750	90.0%	10.0%
7751 and Above	73.9%	26.1%

CHAPTER ELEVEN: WORKSTATION DEVELOPMENT PLANS

A surprisingly high percentage of academic libraries are offering workstations equipped with applications software -- 53.6%. About 41% of libraries plan to offer "holistic" workstations, those that offer both applications software and information services. In general, libraries are reducing their purchases of personal computers, even as personal computer purchases in the student population and in the general public have soared. Personal computer purchases by libraries fell an estimated 20% in 1998. Data on spending for personal computers by libraries is suspect because many libraries receive computers from general college technology budgets rather than library budgets. Also, libraries sometimes receive gifts of computers. In addition, some colleges report bare-bone shell workstations as "personal computers" and others do not. Also, computer purchases tend to be cyclical; a library may spend enormous sums in one year and nothing the next. The lack of uniformity in year to year purchasing introduces more variance into a sample and renders it less accurate.

It is probably necessary to do a detailed survey focused highly specifically on computer hardware purchases to get a really specific idea of what academic libraries are doing in information technology hardware. However, we will say this. In both of our academic library reports in 1996 and 1998, libraries report lower spending on "personal computers." This is exactly what many technology pundits predict for the broader society. As telecommunications-based information processing becomes easier to use and less expensive, workstations that draw programs from the internet may replace desk top personal computers. A variant of this seems to be happening in the academic library which, as stated previously, tends to be a good indicator of what happens later in the broader society.

Table #236: Percentage of Academic Libraries that offer Workstations equipped with Applications Software such as Word Processing, Spreadsheets, or Statistical Packages

	YES	NO
All Libraries	53.6%	46.4%

Table #237: Percentage of Academic Libraries that offer Workstations equipped with Applications Software such as Word Processing, Spreadsheets, or Statistical Packages, Broken out by Type of Control of the School, Public or Private

Type of Control	YES	NO
Private	53.3%	46.7%
Public	52.9%	47.1%

Table #238: Percentage of Academic Libraries that offer Workstations equipped with Applications Software such as Word Processing, Spreadsheets, or Statistical Packages, Broken out by Level of the School, Two-Year or Four-Year

Level of the School	YES	NO
Four-Year	54.2%	45.8%
Two-Year	50.0%	50.0%

Table #239: Percentage of Academic Libraries that offer Workstations equipped with Applications Software such as Word Processing, Spreadsheets, or Statistical Packages, Broken out by Size of the School

Size of the School	YES	NO
1 - 2200	47.8%	52.2%
2201 - 3500	65.4%	34.6%
3501 - 7750	26.1%	73.9%
7751 and Above	71.0%	29.2%

Table #240: Percentage of Academic Libraries that Plan to Develop "Holistic" Workstations that Offer Both Information Services and Applications Software on the Same Workstation

	Yes	No
All Libraries	41.46%	58.54%

Table #241: Percentage of Academic Libraries that Plan to Develop "Holistic" Workstations that Offer Both Information Services and Applications Software on the Same Workstation, Broken out by Type of Control of the School, Public or Private

Type of Control	Yes	No
Public	37.78%	62.23%
Private	45.95%	54.05%

* Note: Numbers may not add up to 100.00 due to rounding

Table #242: Percentage of Academic Libraries that Plan to Develop "Holistic" Workstations that Offer Both Information Services and Applications Software on the Same Workstation, Broken out by Level of the School, Two-Year or Four-Year

Level of the School	Yes	No
Two-Year	38.24%	61.76%
Four-Year	43.75%	56.25%

Table #243: Percentage of Academic Libraries that Plan to Develop "Holistic" Workstations that Offer Both Information Services and Applications Software on the Same Workstation, Broken out by Size of the School

Size of the School	Yes	No
1-2200	45.45%	54.55%
2201-3500	45.00%	55.00%
3501-7750	38.10%	61.90%
7751 and Above	36.84%	63.16%

Table #244: Percentage of Academic Libraries' Workstations that Currently can be Described as "Holistic" Workstations

	Mean Percentage	Median Percentage	Minimum	Maximum
All Libraries	39.68	25.00	0.00	100.00

Table #245: Percentage of Academic Libraries' Workstations that Currently can be Described as "Holistic" Workstations, Broken out by Type of Control of the School, Public or Private

Type of Control	Mean Percentage	Median Percentage	Minimum	Maximum
Public	39.91	25.00	0.00	100.00
Private	39.45	35.00	0.00	100.00

Table #246: Percentage of Academic Libraries' Workstations that Currently can be Described as "Holistic" Workstations, Broken out by Level of the School, Two-Year or Four-Year

Level of the School	Mean Percentage	Median Percentage	Minimum	Maximum
Two-Year	44.92	37.95	0.00	100.00
Four-Year	36.83	25.00	0.00	100.00

Table #247: Percentage of Academic Libraries' Workstations that Currently can be Described as "Holistic" Workstations, Broken out by Size of the School

Size of the School	Mean Percentage	Median Percentage	Minimum	Maximum
1-2200	46.10	58.00	0.00	100.00
2201-3500	41.60	30.00	0.00	100.00
3500-7750	33.70	7.00	0.00	100.00
7751 and Above	35.14	25.00	0.00	100.00

Table #248: Total Number of Personal Computers Purchased by Academic Libraries, 1997-98 and 1998-99

	Mean Number	Median Number	Minimum	Maximum	% Mean Increase
1997-98	15	5	0	150	
1998-99	12	5	0	150	-20.00

Table #249: Mean Number of Personal Computers Purchased by Academic Libraries, Broken out by Type of Control of the School, Public or Private, 1997-98

Type of Control	Mean Number	Median Number	Minimum	Maximum
Public	16	6	0	150
Private	13	5	0	150

Table #250: Mean Number of Personal Computers Purchased by Academic Libraries, Broken out by Level of the School, Two-Year or Four-Year, 1997-98

Level of the School	Mean Number	Median Number	Minimum	Maximum
Two-Year	11	5	0	70
Four-Year	18	6	0	150

Table #251: Mean Number of Personal Computers Purchased by Academic Libraries, Broken out by Size of the School, 1997-98

Size of the School	Mean Number	Median Number	Minimum	Maximum
1-2200	6	4	0	28
2201-3500	7	5	0	60
3501-7750	15	10	0	81
7751 and Above	33	21	0	150

Table #252: Mean Number of Personal Computers Purchased by Academic Libraries, Broken out by Type of Control of the School, Public or Private, 1998-99

Type of Control	Mean Number	Median Number	Minimum	Maximum
Public	15	10	0	150
Private	9	4	0	56

Table #253: Mean Number of Personal Computers Purchased by Academic Libraries, Broken out by Level of the School, Two-Year or Four-Year, 1998-99

Level of the School	Mean Number	Median Number	Minimum	Maximum
Two-Year	11	4	0	56
Four-Year	13	6	0	150

Table #254: Mean Number of Personal Computers Purchased by Academic Libraries, Broken out by Size of the School, 1998-99

Size of the School	Mean Number	Median Number	Minimum	Maximum
1-2200	5	3	0	23
2201-3500	9	4	0	40
3501-7750	8	2	0	30
7751 and Above	27	20	0	150

Primary Research Group, Inc.   **68 W. 38th St., #202, NY, NY 10018**   **(212)764-1579**

CHAPTER TWELVE: DATABASE ACQUISITION TRENDS

Table #255: Percentage of Academic Libraries that Conduct Searches for Themselves or for their Clientele that Frequently Require the Accumulation of Government Statistics and Information

	YES	NO
All Libraries	68.2%	31.8%

Table #256: Percentage of Academic Libraries that Conduct Searches for Themselves of for their Clientele that Frequently Require the Accumulation of Government Statistics and Information, Broken out by Type of Control of the School, Public or Private

Type of Control	YES	NO
Private	65.0%	35.0%
Public	70.2%	29.8%

Table #257: Percentage of Academic Libraries that Conduct Searches for Themselves or for their Clientele that Frequently Require the Accumulation of Government Statistics and Information, Broken out by Level of the School, Two-Year or Four-Year

Level of the School	YES	NO
Two-Year	63.6%	36.4%
Four-Year	70.9%	29.1%

Table #258: Percentage of Academic Libraries that Conduct Searches for Themselves of for their Clientele that Frequently Require the Accumulation of Government Statistics and Information, Broken out by Size of the School

Size of the School	YES	NO
1 - 2200	58.3%	41.7%
2201 - 3500	61.9%	38.1%
3501 - 7750	68.4%	31.6%
7751 and Above	83.3%	16.7%

Table #259: Percentage of Government Statistics and Information Searches Satisfied by Print Sources

	Mean Percentage	Median Percentage	Minimum	Maximum
All Libraries	10.96	1.00	1.00	75.00

Table #260: Percentage of Government Statistics and Information Searches Satisfied by Print Sources, Broken out by Type of Control of the School, Public or Private

Type of Control	Mean Percentage	Median Percentage	Minimum	Maximum
Public	12.84	1.00	1.00	75.00
Private	8.43	1.00	1.00	60.00

Table #261: Percentage of Government Statistics and Information Searches Satisfied by Print Sources, Broken out by Level of the School, Two-Year or Four-Year

Level of the School	Mean Percentage	Median Percentage	Minimum	Maximum
Two-Year	8.89	1.00	1.00	75.00
Four-Year	12.00	1.00	1.00	60.00

Table #262: Percentage of Government Statistics and Information Searches Satisfied by Print Sources, Broken out by Size of the School

Size of the School	Mean Percentage	Median Percentage	Minimum	Maximum
1-2200	10.20	1.00	1.00	60.00
2201-3500	15.31	1.00	1.00	65.00
3501-7750	9.67	1.00	1.00	60.00
7751 and Above	9.00	1.00	1.00	75.00

Table #263: Percentage of Government Statistics and Information Searches Satisfied by CD-ROMs

	Mean Percentage	Median Percentage	Minimum	Maximum
All Libraries	4.79	2.00	0.00	45.00

Table #264: Percentage of Government Statistics and Information Searches Satisfied by CD-ROMs, Broken out by Type of Control of the School, Public or Private

Type of Control	Mean Percentage	Median Percentage	Minimum	Maximum
Public	4.62	2.00	0.00	45.00
Private	5.00	1.00	0.00	40.00

Table #265: Percentage of Government Statistics and Information Searches Satisfied by CD-ROMs, Broken out by Level of the School, Two-Year or Four-Year

Level of the School	Mean Percentage	Median Percentage	Minimum	Maximum
Two-Year	2.44	2.00	1.00	15.00
Four-Year	5.87	1.00	0.00	45.00

Table #266: Percentage of Government Statistics and Information Searches Satisfied by CD-ROMs, Broken out by Size of the School

Size of the School	Mean Percentage	Median Percentage	Minimum	Maximum
1-2200	1.80	1.00	0.00	10.00
2201-3500	10.86	2.00	0.00	45.00
3501-7750	4.82	2.00	1.00	30.00
7751 and Above	2.41	1.00	1.00	10.00

Primary Research Group, Inc.   **68 W. 38th St., #202, NY, NY 10018**   **(212)764-1579**

Table #267: Percentage of Government Statistics and Information Searches Satisfied by On-Line Services

	Mean Percentage	Median Percentage	Minimum	Maximum
All Libraries	2.39	1.00	0.00	30.00

Table #268: Percentage of Government Statistics and Information Searches Satisfied by On-Line Services, Broken out by Type of Control of the School, Public or Private

Type of Control	Mean Percentage	Median Percentage	Minimum	Maximum
Public	2.71	1.00	0.00	30.00
Private	1.96	2.00	0.00	10.00

Table #269: Percentage of Government Statistics and Information Searches Satisfied by On-Line Services, Broken out by Level of the School, Two-Year or Four-Year

Level of the School	Mean Percentage	Median Percentage	Minimum	Maximum
Two-Year	1.28	1.00	0.00	2.00
Four-Year	2.94	1.00	0.00	30.00

Table #270: Percentage of Government Statistics and Information Searches Satisfied by On-Line Services, Broken out by Size of the School

Size of the School	Mean Percentage	Median Percentage	Minimum	Maximum
1-2200	3.93	2.00	0.00	30.00
2201-3500	1.42	1.00	0.00	5.00
3501-7750	1.40	1.50	0.00	2.00
7751 and Above	2.29	1.00	1.00	20.00

Table #271: Percentage of Government Statistics and Information Searches Satisfied by Government On-Line Services

	Mean Percentage	Median Percentage	Minimum	Maximum
All Libraries	4.63	1.00	0.00	100.00

Table #272: Percentage of Government Statistics and Information Searches Satisfied by Government On-Line Services, Broken out by Type of Control of the School, Public or Private

Type of Control	Mean Percentage	Median Percentage	Minimum	Maximum
Public	2.50	1.00	0.00	30.00
Private	7.22	1.00	0.00	100.00

Table #273: Percentage of Government Statistics and Information Searches Satisfied by Government On-Line Services, Broken out by Level of the School, Two-Year or Four-Year

Level of the School	Mean Percentage	Median Percentage	Minimum	Maximum
Two-Year	1.73	2.00	1.00	5.00
Four-Year	5.83	1.00	0.00	100.00

Table #274: Percentage of Government Statistics and Information Searches Satisfied by Government On-Line Services, Broken out by Size of the College

Size of the School	Mean Percentage	Median Percentage	Minimum	Maximum
1-2200	1.73	1.00	0.00	10.00
2201-3501	13.18	2.00	0.00	100.00
3501-7750	4.20	1.50	0.00	30.00
7751 and Above	1.53	1.00	1.00	5.00

Table #275: Percentage of Government Statistics and Information Searches Satisfied by the Internet

	Mean Percentage	Median Percentage	Minimum	Maximum
All Libraries	7.74	1.00	1.00	80.00

Table #276: Percentage of Government Statistics and Information Searches Satisfied by the Internet, Broken out by Type of Control of the School, Public or Private

Type of Control	Mean Percentage	Median Percentage	Minimum	Maximum
Public	7.78	1.00	1.00	50.00
Private	7.68	1.00	1.00	80.00

Table #277: Percentage of Government Statistics and Information Searches Satisfied by the Internet, Broken out by Level of the College, Two-Year or Four-Year

Level of the School	Mean Percentage	Median Percentage	Minimum	Maximum
Two-Year	3.11	1.00	1.00	25.00
Four-Year	9.87	1.00	1.00	80.00

Table #278: Percentage of Government Statistics and Information Searches Satisfied by the Internet, Broken out by Size of the School

Size of the School	Mean Percentage	Median Percentage	Minimum	Maximum
1-2200	7.47	1.00	1.00	50.00
2201-3500	10.38	2.00	1.00	40.00
3501-7750	5.36	1.00	1.00	30.00
7751 and Above	7.50	1.00	1.00	80.00

Table #279: Percentage of Academic Libraries that Plan to Increase Use of CD-ROM as a Form of Database Retrieval

	YES	NO
All Libraries	34.2%	65.8%

Table #280: Percentage of Academic Libraries that Plan to Increase Use of CD-ROM as a Form of Database Retrieval, Broken out by Type of Control of the School, Public or Private

Type of Control	YES	NO
Public	37.2%	62.8%
Private	30.6%	69.4%

Table #281: Percentage of Academic Libraries that Plan to Increase Use of CD-ROM as a Form of Database Retrieval, Broken out by Level of the School, Two-Year or Four-Year

Level of the School	YES	NO
Two-Year	41.4%	58.6%
Four-Year	30.0%	70.0%

Table #282: Percentage of Academic Libraries that Plan to Increase Use of CD-ROM as a Form of Database Retrieval, Broken out by Size of the School

Size of the School	YES	NO
1 - 2200	39.1%	60.9%
2201 - 3500	26.3%	73.7%
3501 - 7750	37.5%	62.5%
7751 and Above	33.3%	66.7%

Table #283: Percentage of Academic Libraries that Plan to Increase Use of Magnetic Tape as a Form of Database Retrieval

	Yes	No
All Libraries	2.53%	97.47%

Table #284: Percentage of Academic Libraries that Plan to Increase Use of Magnetic Tape as a Form of Database Retrieval, Broken out by Type of Control of the School, Public or Private

Type of Control	Yes	No
Public	0.00%	100.00%
Private	5.56%	94.44%

Table #285: Percentage of Academic Libraries that Plan to Increase Use of Magnetic Tape as a Form of Database Retrieval, Broken out by Level of the School, Two-Year or Four-Year

Level of the School	Yes	No
Two-Year	0.00%	100.00%
Four-Year	4.00%	96.00%

Table #286: Percentage of Academic Libraries that Plan to Increase Use of Magnetic Tape as a Form of Database Retrieval, Broken out by Size of the School

Size of the School	Yes	No
1-2200	4.35%	95.65%
2201-3500	5.26%	94.74%
3501-7750	0.00%	100.00%
7751 and Above	0.00%	100.00%

Table #287: Percentage of Academic Libraries that Plan to Increase Use of Commercial On-Line Services as a Form of Database Retrieval

	Yes	No
All Libraries	64.56%	35.44%

Primary Research Group, Inc.   **68 W. 38th St., #202, NY, NY 10018**   **(212)764-1579**

Table #288: Percentage of Academic Libraries that Plan to Increase Use of Commercial On-Line Services as a Form of Database Retrieval, Broken out by Type of Control of the School, Public or Private

Type of Control	Yes	No
Public	62.79%	37.21%
Private	66.67%	33.34%

* Note: Numbers may not add up to 100.00 due to rounding

Table #289: Percentage of Academic Libraries that Plan to Increase Use of Commercial On-Line Services as a Form of Database Retrieval, Broken out by Level of the School, Two-Year or Four-Year

Level of the School	Yes	No
Two-Year	62.07%	37.93%
Four-Year	66.00%	34.00%

Table #290: Percentage of Academic Libraries that Plan to Increase Use of Commercial On-Line Services as a Form of Database Retrieval, Broken out by Size of the School

Size of the School	Yes	No
1-2200	60.87%	39.13%
2201-3500	52.63%	47.37%
3501-7750	68.75%	31.25%
7751 and Above	76.19%	23.81%

Table #291: Percentage of Academic Libraries that Plan to Increase Use of the Internet as a Form of Database Retrieval

	YES	NO
All Libraries	97.4%	2.60%

Table #292: Percentage of Academic Libraries that Plan to Increase Use of the Internet as a Form of Database Retrieval, Broken out by Type of Control of the School, Public or Private

Type of Control	YES	NO
Public	100.0%	0.0%
Private	94.3%	5.7%

Table #293: Percentage of Academic Libraries that Plan to Increase Use of the Internet as a Form of Database Retrieval, Broken out by Level of the School, Two-Year or Four-Year

Level of the School	YES	NO
Two-Year	100.0%	0.0%
Four-Year	95.9%	4.1%

Table #294: Percentage of Academic Libraries that Plan to Increase Use of the Internet as a Form of Database Retrieval, Broken out by Size of the School

Size of the School	YES	NO
1 - 2200	95.7%	4.4%
2201 - 3500	94.7%	5.3%
3501 - 7750	100.0%	0.0%
7751 and Above	100.0%	0.0%

Table #295: Perceived Consequences of Increased Familiarity with the Internet: Internet usage substituted for commercial on-line usage; both internet and commercial on-line usage increased; both; or neither.

	Substitute Internet Usage	Increase Internet and Commercial On-Line Usage	Neither	Both
All Libraries	23.08	55.13	12.82	8.97

Table #296: Perceived Consequences of Increased Familiarity with the Internet: Internet usage substituted for commercial on-line usage; both internet and commercial on-line usage increased; both; or neither. Broken out by Type of Control of the School, Public or Private.

Type of Control	Substitute Internet Usage	Increase Internet and Commercial Usage	Neither	Both
Public	17.78	62.23	13.34	6.67
Private	30.30	45.46	12.12	12.12

* Note: Numbers may not add up to 100.00 due to rounding

Table #297: Perceived Consequences of Increased Familiarity with the Internet: Internet usage substituted for commercial on-line usage; both internet and commercial on-line usage increased; both; or neither. Broken out by Level of the School, Two-Year or Four-Year.

Level of the School	Substituted Internet Usage	Increased Internet and Commercial Usage	Neither	Both
Two-Year	16.67	66.67	16.67	0.00
Four-Year	27.08	47.92	10.42	14.58

* Note: Numbers may not add up to 100.00 due to rounding

Table #298: Perceived Consequences of Increased Familiarity with the Internet: Internet usage substituted for commercial on-line usage; both internet and commercial on-line usage increased; both; or neither. Broken out by Size of the School.

Size of the School	Substituted Internet for Commercial Usage	Increased Internet and Commercial Usage	Neither	Both
1-2200	17.39	52.17	17.39	13.04
2201-3500	33.34	40.00	13.34	13.34
3501-7750	35.29	58.82	5.88	0.00
7751 and Above	13.04	65.22	13.04	8.70

* Note: Numbers may not add up to 100.00 due to rounding

APPENDIX A: OPEN-ENDED QUESTIONS

Has the library, to any extent, reduced commercial on-line usage, by substituting information obtained for free over the internet?

The library's database search strategies don't often access information on the internet that is available without a fee in place of information that was once purchased through an on-line service. "We answer many quick reference questions with the internet. More detailed bibliographic lists still require either an on-line service or a CD-ROM." - Public, Four-Year School with 2200 students or fewer

No. Students are neglecting print sources, though, we need to educate them that if they don't find what they are looking for on-line there are other resources out there. - Private, Four-Year School with between 2201 and 3500 students

No. We really haven't reduced the on-line commercial databases, because through the consortium access to on-line database has increased. So, we haven't had to. - Private, Four-Year School with 2200 students or fewer

Not really. There's a lot of stuff out there on the internet and a lot of it is just stuff. We really encourage our students to use legitimate sources, but it doesn't mean there not using the stuff. - Public, Two-Year School with between 3501 and 7750 students

No, moving towards full text, cannot get that over the internet. - Private, Four-Year School with between 3501 and 7750 students

No, the library has not reduced commercial on-line usage, by substituting information obtained for free over the internet. - Private, Four-Year School with between 3501 and 7750 students

The library has reduced commercial on-line usage, by substituting information obtained for free over the internet. "We have eliminated on-line access to NLM as a paid database. - Public, Four-Year School with between 3500 and 7751 students

The library hasn't reduced commercial on-line usage by substituting information obtained for free over the internet. "We haven't gotten rid of anything, just added it on." - Private, Four-Year School with 2200 students or fewer

The library hasn't reduced commercial on-line usage by substituting information obtained for free over the internet. "The greater impact has been loading our CD-ROM commercial databases in a networked pc environment. - Public, Four-Year School with 7751 students or more

The library isn't reducing commercial on-line usage by substituting information obtained for free over the internet. "We are still adding commercial on-line services and augmenting with free internet information." - Private, Four-Year School with between 2201 and 3500 students

"No!!!" The library has not reduced commercial on-line usage by substituting information obtained for free over the internet. "Some Internet 'free' information is supplemental, but 95% is poor quality, non-reviewed, which makes it useless for research. - Private, Four-Year School with 2200 students or fewer

Yes, the library has reduced commercial on-line usage: "the State of Missouri pays for EBSCOhost Masterfile." - Public, Two-Year School with 2200 students or fewer

No, the library hasn't substituted paid access over the internet for paid access to traditional on-line services, like Dialog. - Private, Four-Year School with between 2201 and 3500 students

The library hasn't to any extent reduced commercial on-line usage by substituting information obtained for free over the internet. "I think we pay for most of them." - Private, Four-Year School with between 2201 and 3500 students

The library hasn't, to any extent, reduced commercial on-line usage, by substituting information obtained for free over the internet. The library has, in fact, been doing the opposite by increasing licensing. - Private, Four-Year School with between 2201 and 3500 students

The library has, to some extent, reduced commercial on-line usage, by substituting information obtained for free over the internet. The library uses the free stuff when it comes to finances, but it's not as reliable as commercial usage, so it doesn't take the place of commercial usage. - Private, Four-Year School with between 2201 and 3500 students

The library accesses both the South Carolina Discus Program and Britannica On-line through the internet. - Private, Four-Year School with 2200 students or fewer

The library has, to some extent, reduced commercial on-line usage, by substituting information obtained for free over the internet. The library has done this in the area of business, because those stats are available on-line. - Private, Four-Year School with 7751 students or more

The library hasn't to any extent reduced commercial on-line usage by substituting information obtained for free over the internet because the library's commercial on-line usage is paid for by the Kansas State Library. - Public, Two-Year School with between 2201 and 3500 students

The library has "somewhat" reduced commercial on-line usage, by substituting info. obtained via the Internet. "We have accessed stock quotes via the web, for example, instead of using Dialog. More commonly we have cut print products in favor of Internet resources, e.g. Thomas Register of American Manufacturers, N.A.D.A Used Car Buying Guide, pamphlet file items. - Private, Four-Year School with between 3501 and 7750 students

An additional 18 libraries simply replied no, they haven't reduced commercial on-line usage by substituting information obtained for free over the internet; 5 replied yes, they have; and 2 stated that they have, but only to a very small degree.

If you have used this option [internet access option offered by major commercial on-line vendors], comment on why and how often you access through the internet commercial databases instead of accessing these databases through the traditional on-line channel connections offered by these publishers.

It's less expensive, though it is sometimes slower, but it still saves more money. - Private, Four-Year School with between 3501 and 7750 students

We do access them offered by the publishers, like Search Bank.   Lexis Nexus is an example of one that we use to pay. We use both because, there are not enough free ones that are good. You can't tell me there is a Lexis Nexus that is free. - Public, Four-Year School with between 3501 and 7750 students

We haven't used dial up for 7 years. - Public, Four-Year School with 7751 students or more

We use Information Access, which is like Infotrack, it's a journal index. Some is full text. We access it through the internet because it's more easily available to our students that way. - Private, Four-Year School with between 2201 and 3500 students

Not to a large extent yet. We find that particularly remote users find the web based products easier to use. - Public, Four-Year School with between 3501 and 7750 students

Easier to use. - Public, Two-Year School with between 2201 and 3500 students

More and more frequently, but on a trial basis. We subscribe for a year to test and then we change database for lack of use. - Public, Four-Year School with 7751 students or more

It's faster and more convenient. - Public, Two-Year School with between 2201 and 3500 students

It's easy. - Public, Four-Year School with between 3501 and 7750 students

We don't have to worry about updates. It's also more timely. - Private, Four-Year School with 2200 or fewer students

Site licenses. - Private, Four-Year School with between 3501 and 7750 students

We do it because of cost, the reason we don't do it more is because of reliability, it doesn't always work. We'd like to go through the internet more, but sometimes it just doesn't work because of technical problems. - Private, Four-Year College with 2200 students or fewer

Our new catalog system is web based, so it is easy access. - Private, Four-Year School with 7751 students or more

It's cheaper, we do it exclusively. - Public, Two-Year School with between 3501 and 7750 students

1000's of times a year. We have the illusion that it's less expensive, but if you figure in people's times waiting for stuff on the internet. There are a lot of problems. It's not reliable. The time of day makes a difference. People get frustrated and wasted their time, I consider that a great expense. - Private, Four-Year School with between 2201 and 3500 students

It's easier to make it available to campus network. - Private, Four-Year School with between 2201 and 3500 students

The ones we get don't offer it. - Private, Four-Year School with 2200 or fewer students

Accessible to everyone. - Private, Four-Year School with between 2201 and 3500 students

Because of the easy access. - Public, Four-Year School with 7751 students or more

The library has used the internet access option offered by major commercial on-line vendors to access for-pay commercial databases instead of accessing these databases through the traditional on-line channel connections offered by these publishers because it is "more economical, more accessible, more long-term, and user friendly." - Private, Four-Year School with between 2201 and 3500 students

The library has used the internet access option offered by major commercial on-line vendors to access for-pay commercial databases through the internet. "We only used on-line searching for specialized databases, for searches done by a librarian. These are databases we do not need full time, but only occasionally." - Public, Four-Year School with between 3501 and 7750 students

The library accesses commercial databases through the internet instead of through the traditional on-line channel connections offered by the publishers because of a state-wide consortium of database access. - Public, Four-Year School with 2200 students or fewer

The library accesses for-pay commercial databases through the internet instead of through the traditional on-line channel connections offered by the publishers because "accessibility is easier and the search engines are better designed." - Public, Four-Year School with 7751 students or more

The library has used the internet access option offered by major commercial on-line vendors to access for-pay commercial databases through the internet because of cost. - Public, Two-Year School with between 2201 and 3500 students

The library has used the internet access option offered by major commercial on-line vendors to access for-pay commercial databases through the internet because, "it's free!" - Private, Four-Year School with 2200 students or fewer

The library has used the internet access option offered by major commercial on-line vendors to access for-pay commercial databases through the internet because, "the Internet 'tends' to offer a common access point familiar to all patrons, although it often gives up interface options." - Private, Four-Year School with 2200 students or fewer

The library has used the internet access option offered by major commercial on-line vendors to access for-pay commercial databases through the internet because, "pay per use through FirstSearch (OCLC) allows us access to many databases we couldn't otherwise use. We don't use this service regularly." - Private, Four-Year School with 2200 students or fewer

Yes, the library has used the internet access option offered by major commercial on-line vendors to access for-pay commercial databases through the internet, because access is more flexible, and more end-user friendly. - Private, Four-Year School with between 2201 and 3500 students

The library has used the internet access option offered by major commercial on-line vendors to access for-pay commercial databases through the internet. The library says, "It's hazy weather, we get subscriptions for full-text database through the internet. We use EBSCOhost, they're a major vendor." - Private, Four-Year School with 2200 students or fewer

The library has used the internet access option offered by major commercial on-line vendors to access for-pay commercial databases through the internet. The library has a fixed-fee subscription, so rather than do per hour access through the traditional on-line connections, the library goes through the internet. - Public, Four-Year School with 7751 students or more

The library has used the internet access option offered by major commercial on-line vendors to access for-pay commercial databases through the internet. The library finds this much easier and more convenient. - Private, Four-Year School with 2200 students or fewer

The library has used the internet access option offered by major commercial on-line vendors to access for-pay commercial databases through the internet because it "offers greater access via the Internet and computer terminals." 1998 will be the library's first year of access. - Public, Two-Year School with 7751 students or more

On using the internet access option offered by major commercial on-line vendors to access for-pay commercial databases through the internet, the library says it does because it offers easier access. - Private, Four-Year School with between 3501 and 7750 students

The library accesses commercial databases through the internet instead of through the traditional on-line channel connections offered by the publishers because of a state-wide consortium of database access. - Public, Two-Year School with 7751 students or more

The library has used the internet access option offered by major commercial on-line vendors to access for-pay commercial databases through the internet, because of convenience. - Public, Two-Year School with between 3501 and 7750 students

The library has used the internet access option offered by major commercial on-line vendors to access for-pay commercial databases through the internet, when using the Kansas State Library's provision of FirstSearch database. - Public, Two-Year School with between 2201 and 3500 students

The library has used the internet access option offered by major commercial on-line vendors to access for-pay commercial databases through the internet, because it saves a little bit of money and it offers a faster data rate. - Public, Two-Year School with 7751 students or more

The library has used the internet access option offered by major commercial on-line vendors to access for-pay commercial databases through the internet, because it offers greater ease of access. - Public, Two-Year School with 7751 students or more

The library has used the internet access option offered by major commercial on-line vendors to access for-pay commercial databases through the internet, because it is faster. - Private, Four-Year School with between 2201 and 3500 students

The library has used the internet access option offered by major commercial on-line vendors to access for-pay commercial databases through the internet, because it is trying to migrate resources to the web. - Private, Four-Year School with between 3501 and 7750 students

The library has used the internet access option offered by major commercial on-line vendors to access for-pay commercial databases through the internet, because it offers better service and reduces the cost. We use this option everyday. - Private, Two-Year School with 7751 students or more

The library has used the internet access option offered by major commercial on-line vendors to access for-pay commercial databases through the internet because of "convenience." - Public, Four-Year School with 2200 students or fewer

How many CD-ROM database subscriptions does the library have? Please list them:

The answers to this question revealed an interesting trend when compared to survey responses from 1991 and 1996, found in the 1996 edition of *The Academic Library Budget & Expenditure Report*. In 1991, librarians had fewer options in terms of CD-ROM databases, and thus a few companies commanded a large percentage of the CD-ROM database market. However, as the decade progressed, and options grew, librarians have drawn on an increasingly wide selection of CD-ROM databases. Many of the same companies still lead the CD-ROM database market, but the market share of each has decreased since 1991.

The 1991 survey of academic libraries in four-year colleges and universities found that the leading CD-ROM titles were largely the same as in two-year and four-year colleges and universities in 1998: ERIC. InfoTrac, Psychlit, ABI-INFORM, the Academic Index, Medline, and CINAHL. These seven titles accounted for 40 percent of the titles listed.

CD-ROM Titles to which Academic Libraries Subscribed -- 1991

CD-ROM Title	Total Number Found in Sample
ERIC	61
Infotrac	39
Psychlit	33
ABI-INFORM	20
Academic Index	19
Medline	15
Cinahl	14
Social Science Cit. Index	13
UMI*	12
Compact Disclosure	11
Books In Print	11
Newsbank	11
Business Periodical Index	10
Wilson (particular product not identified)	9
MLA International	8
Humanities Index	8
PAIS (Public Affairs Information Service)	7
Reader's Guide To Periodical Literature	7
Compustat Index Plus	7
CIRR (Corporate & Industry Research Reports)	7

As the nineties progressed, librarians found that they had a broader selection of CD-ROM titles from which to choose. In 1996, though the leading companies were largely the same as in 1991, each accounted for a smaller percentage of the total market.

CD-ROM Titles to which Academic Libraries Subscribed -- 1996

CD-ROM Title	Total Number Found in Sample
ERIC	22
ProQuest	13
Medline	12
Newsbank	12
American Business Disc	11
InfoTrac	11
Psychlit	8
ABI-INFORM	7
Academic Abstracts	7
MLA Bibliograpy	7
National Trade Data Bank	7
New York Times	7
Academic Index	6
Encyclopedia Britannica	6
Prophone	6
American History and Life	5
CAB Abstracts	4
CINAHL	4
County Buisiness Patterns	4
Newspaper Abstracts	4

The leading titles remained more or less constant through 1998, though there have been notable changes in the market share commanded by each. Again, due largely to the broader selection of titles, each accounted for a smaller share of the total market than in 1991.

CD-ROM Titles to which Academic Libraries Subscribe -- 1998

CD-ROM Title	Total Number Found in Sample
CINAHL	22
ERIC	18
Books in Print	14
Newsbank	14
Infotrac	13
MLA	13
SIRS	12
Academic Abstracts	10
Psychlit	10
American History and Life	7
GPO	7
New York Times	6
Sociofile	6
Sport Disc	6
ATLA Religion Index	5
Social Science Index	5
Ethnic News Watch	4
HAPI	4
Medline	4
Reader's Guide Abstracts	4

In your database search strategies, do you find that you often access information on the internet that is available without a fee in place of information that you once purchased through a commercial on-line service? Please comment.

"Our main campus is utilizing "distance learning" dollars to mount databases for remote use. This is the largest benefit we have received from the internet." - Public, Four-Year School with 2200 students or fewer

The library doesn't often accesses free information that it once paid for via commercial vendors. "We pay for the delivery of many databases previously accessed on CD or on-line. What we get free generally doesn't overlap; ERIC is one exception." - Private, Four-Year School with between 3501 and 7750 students

Yes. The library often accesses free information on the internet, in place of information purchased through a commercial on-line service. The library goes to the free information first. - Private, Two-Year School with 7751 students or more

The library "sometimes" accesses free information "in addition to" information paid for via commercial vendors. - Private, Four-Year School with between 2201 and 3500 students

Yes. The library's database search strategies often access information on the internet that is available without a fee in place of information that was once purchased through an on-line service. "We do not use commercial sources." - Public, Two-Year School with between 2201 and 3500 students

The library does sometimes access free information that it once paid for via commercial vendors, but only through NCM and ERIC. - Public, Four-Year School with between 3501 and 7750 students

The library seldom accesses information on the internet that is available without a fee in place of another place to look--sometimes better, sometimes poorer. - Private, Four-Year School with between 2201 and 3500 students

Accessing information on the internet is supplemental to information we access through on-line services. - Public, Four-Year School with 7751 students or more

In the library's database search strategies, they have dropped searches such as DIALOG as the library doesn't need them. - Private, Four-Year School with between 3501 and 7750 students

Almost never does the library access information on the internet that is available without a fee, in place of information that was once purchased through an on-line service. "Fee based information is more quality controlled." - Private, Four-Year School with 2200 students or fewer

Yes, the library often finds that in its database search strategies, it accesses information on the Internet that is available without a fee in place of information that you once purchased through a commercial on-line service. For example, when looking for books in print, patrons check Amazon.com or Barnes&Noble.com. Also used is the Thomas Register, for zip codes, addresses and phone numbers. - Public, Two-Year School with 2200 students or fewer

Sometimes, in database search strategies the library accesses information on the internet that is available without a fee in place of information that was once purchased through a commercial on-line service. But, usually the library has to subscribe for valuable information. - Private, Four-Year School with between 2201 and 3500 students

No, in its database search strategies the library doesn't often find that it accesses information on the internet that is available without a fee in place of information that was once purchased through a commercial on-line service. "At this point finding certain information through commercial services can be more expedient." - Private, Two-Year School with 2200 students or fewer

In the library's database search strategies, the library finds that they often access information on the internet that is available without a fee in place of information that was once purchased through a commercial on-line service. "We do that more often now, but even still, I'm not sure if we use free internet information more than what we pay for." - Private, Four-Year School with between 2201 and 3500 students

In the library's database search strategies the library finds that they often access information on the internet that is available without a fee in place of information that it once purchased through a commercial on-line service. "We're so new at it we just got our computers up and running this summer. So, we're thinking that students do do that." - Private, Four-Year School with 2200 students or fewer

Occasionally, in the library's database search strategies, the library accesses information on the internet that is available without a fee, from non-profit sites, in place of information that it once purchased through a commercial on-line service. - Private, Four-Year School with between 2201 and 3500 students

In its database search strategies the library doesn't depend on information accessed through the internet. The library prefers FirstSearch Database because it can be depended on; "it's authoritative." - Public, Two-Year School with 2200 students or fewer

In its database search strategies the library tries to find information on the internet that is available without a fee, to replace information that is purchased though a commercial on-line service. More and more the library is finding that it is able to do this. - Public, Two-Year School with 2200 students or fewer

In its database search strategies the library finds that it often accesses information on the internet, but doesn't replace information accessed through a commercial on-line service with free internet information. - Public, Four-Year School with between 3501 and 7750 students

In the library's database search strategies it finds that it doesn't often access information through the internet that is available without a fee in place of information that was once purchased through a commercial on-line service. Only if material is unavailable elsewhere and is verifiable research does the library use free internet information. - Public, Two-Year School with 7751 students or more

In the library's database search strategies it doesn't find that it often accesses information on the internet that is available without a fee in place of information that it once purchased through a commercial on-line service. "Our experience with commercial on-line services is very limited." - Public, Four-Year School with between 2201 and 3500 students

Yes. It seems a lot of stuff are becoming free, like the phone database. - Private, Four-Year School with between 3501 and 7750 students

Yes. There's just stuff in there you can find for free. You can get stocks and companies and company history on the internet, that's why we're going to drop our value line CD subscription. - Public, Two-Year School with between 3501 and 7750 students

Not often, but some government docs this happens with. - Public, Two-Year School with between 3351 and 7750 students

I think that the stuff available is not all that great. The stuff that people really need, you have to pay for. There's no such thing as a free lunch. - Public, Two-Year School with between 2201 and 3500 students

Yeah, as a matter of fact, we stopped subscribing to the microfiche of college catalogs, because we can get that over the net. And some government documents. And even though we still buy ERIC we're going more towards the web based that is free. - Public, Four-Year School with between 3501 and 7750 students

Yes, we find a lot of business and government information and even news. - Private, Four-Year School with between 2201 and 3500 students

Yes. It's cost effective when it's free on the internet. - Private, Four-Year School with 2200 students or fewer

What is your best purchase that your library has ever made, and why was it such a good purchase? Your answer can include any kind of library oriented product.

The best purchase the library made in terms of equipment was a "CD-ROM database." This allows patrons to learn searching strategy which has now become so important in using the internet effectively." - Public, Four-Year School with 2200 students or fewer

The best purchase the library made in terms of equipment was an "on-line periodical service, EBSCO." - Public, Two-Year School with between 2201 and 3500 students

The best purchase the library ever made was EBSCOhost because of its full text it's "hugely popular." - Private, Four-Year School with between 3501 and 7750 students

The best purchase the library ever made was periodical access via the Internet. - Private, Four-Year School with between 2201 and 3500 students

The best purchase the library ever made was "networking the campus and the sites." - Private, Four-Year School with between 2201 and 3500 students

The best purchase the library has ever made is an "integrated library system, which eliminated some duplication, added serials to the catalog, enabled access outside the library , enabled more authority control, automated some parts of the library and all jobs, and raised visibility, perceived efficiency on campus." - Public, Four-Year School with between 3501 and 7750 students

The best purchase the library has ever made is Innovative Interface on-line LIB INF SYSTEM; user-friendly forms the basis of much of our transition to the on-line library to date. - Public, Four-Year School with 7751 students or more

The best purchase the library ever made was the Novel network. "It was the back bone that made everything else possible. Web access put all the products and catalog together in every machine and made it available off site. - Private, Four-Year School with between 2201 and 3500 students

The best purchase the library has made is shelving. - Public, Four-Year School with between 3501 and 7750 students

The best purchase the library has ever made was an on-line catalog. - Public, Four-Year School with 2200 students or fewer

The best purchase the library has made is an automation system; it simplified many library processes and allowed staff and faculty to catch up on other work. - Private, Four-Year School with 2200 students or fewer

"Broadly, our best purchases are those to access information resources electronically--FirstSearch, IAC journal indexes, Lexis/Nexus, and those through the Florida Center for Library Automation. Because users have access any time, from any place, through our home to information, including full-text. - Public, Four-Year School with 7751 students or more

One of the best purchases the library has made is the on-line service, OCLC FirstSearch, because it "offered a greatly expanded capability to information with very easy searching for students. It was a great asset when we first purchased the searches." Another of the best purchases the library has made is compact shelving for periodicals. "[It] saved a great deal of space, provided expanded space, [and] provided improved access to our journals." - Private, Four-Year School with 2200 students or fewer

Lexis Nexus, because it's frequently used. - Public, Four-Year School with 7751 students or more

Aerial / Software for inter library loan. We now can communicate digitally with other librarians. It's made it so much easier. - Private, Four-Year School with between 2201 and 3500 students

Joining the S. Dakota Library network. It gives us access to a whole lot more information than we could normally afford. - Private, Four-Year School with 2200 students or fewer

The computers, but they came to the computer center. Joining Ohio-Link. We paid 220,000 for a 5 year membership. On products, in general we get an enormous discount. At least 50%. It varies by product. Lexis Nexus, we originally paid $40,000 for it, now as a member of OhioLink we pay $6,000. - Private, Four-Year School with between 3501 and 7750 students

Just purchasing computers and software for our on-line catalog. The on-line catalog does so much for the students. The computer has changed our work situation tremendously in the last five to ten years. - Public, Two-Year School with between 3501 and 7750 students

The single best purchase was our LAN system, included in the Local Area Network (LAN) was SIRS researcher. It was very cost effective because we got so many journals. - Private, Four-Year School with 2200 students or fewer

FirstSearch. It significantly helped. - Private, Four-Year School with between 2201 and 3500 students

EBSCO Host coverage, full text for, relatively speaking, not a lot of money. - Public, Four-Year School with 7751 students or more

The best purchase was the human resources, because without people interpreting resources the library is a jungle of inscrutability and will ever be that. Besides the shortest distance from an answer to a question is always a human resource. - Private, Four-Year School with between 2201 and 3500 students

The on-line databases, we maximize the use of our workstations. - Public, Two-Year School with between 3501 and 7750 students

Encyclopedia Judaica CD ROM, high usage, has an edge over print. - Private, Four-Year School with 2200 students or fewer

Internet access on two computers. - Public, Two-Year School with between 2201 and 3500 students

Our on-line system, because it makes it easier to manage the entire library. - Public, Two-Year School with between 3501 and 7750 students

NC Live. We didn't purchase it, but great acquisition. - Public, Two-Year School with 2200 students or fewer

New integrated library system. Old system ran on mainframe, now it's web based. - Private, Four-Year School with 7751 students or more

Integrated on-line system, because it pulls all the various pieces together from the various systems and makes it much easier to manage. Electronic over mechanical. And you can rethink what you have done and do it differently. - Private, Four-Year School with 2200 students or fewer

Bought very good book scanners. They help with ILL (Inter Library Loans). - Private, Four-Year School with 2200 students or fewer

Catalog System moved from paper. - Private, Four-Year School with between 3501 and 7750 students

The subscription to UMI's ProQuest Direct. It's accessible on-line, we can cover remote sites with it--extension centers for the library--one is 45 miles away, one is 80 miles away. Branches in other parts of the service. - Public, Two-Year School with between 2201 and 3500 students

The server for the network. It provides us with the capability to access information and a network to communicate internally and give catalog access outside the library. - Public, Four-Year School with 7751 students or more

Integrated library catalog system. - Public, Two-Year School with between 2201 and 3500 students

Truthfully, it was the carpet, but . . . the best purchase ever? Well, we've been really excited about the academic index, and we're excited that the Sport Discus is available over the web. So, having the web is the best. - Public, Four-Year School between 3501 and 7750 students

ProQuest subscription providing students with full text. - Public, Two-Year School with 7751 students or more

FirstSearch, because it has so much available under the same search strategy, it has the same interface for so many different databases. - Private, Four-Year School with between 2201 and 3500 students

Infotrack's Academic service, get a lot of use. - Public, Four-Year School with 7751 students or more

Business Newsbank, because it's easy to use and it covers sources that we would have trouble finding otherwise and we are a business school. It covers the regional business newspapers around the country, that would be difficult to get hold of otherwise. - Private, Four-Year School with 2200 students or fewer

Multimedia Instructional classrooms, $47,000 in renovations, upgraded computers and knocked wall out. - Private, Four-Year School with between 3501 and 7750 students

The best purchase the library has ever made was Ebsco's Academic Abstracts, because of its full text. - Public, Two-Year School with 7751 students or more

The best purchase the library has ever made was a CD-ROM juke box, because it increased patron access. - Public, Two-Year School with between 2201 and 3500 students

The best purchase the library has ever made was the on-line service EBSCOhost, because it has so much available from so many places. - Private, Four-Year School with 2200 students or fewer

One of the best purchases the library has made was innovative software for their SWITCH consortium. Another of the best purchases was Infotrac and its many searches. - Private, Four-Year School with between 3501 and 7750 students

The best purchase the library has ever made was staff. "Without trained and experienced staff the resources, regardless of format, would have little or no value in the educational process." - Private, Four-Year School with 2200 students or fewer

The best purchase that the library has ever made is Internet access. - Public, Two-Year School with 2200 students or fewer

The best purchase the library has ever made was a good service-oriented staff with OCLC FirstSearch a very distant second. - Private, Four-Year School with between 2201 and 3500 students

The best purchase that the library ever made was SIRS. It works because you have so many topics, and a variety of sources with the ability to print or download full text. - Private, Two-Year School with 2200 students or fewer

The best purchase that the library has ever made was PCs, because they helped move the library into the information age, starting with dedicated workstations and evolving into networked stations. They introduced the library staff to the necessities of automation, suggested the possibilities of really rapid information retrieval, and prevented the library from becoming an anachronism in its own time!" - Public, Four-Year School with between 2201 and 3500 students

The best purchase the library has ever made is computers, because this has enabled students to have access to the internet. "Even though we don't know how much this has helped them, we know this is what they want." - Private, Four-Year School with 2200 students or fewer

The best purchase the library has ever made was OVID on-line serial index. - Private, Four-Year School with between 2201 and 3500 students

The best purchase the library ever made was ProQuest direct, it gives access to an index of 5,000 full-text journals. - Private, Four-Year School with between 2201 and 3500 students

The best purchase the library has ever made was automating the library and having Opec stations. - Private, Four-Year School with 2200 students or fewer

The best purchase that the library actually paid money for was SIRS Renaissance. While the library didn't spend any money to become a member of the statewide network, which acted to replace a great deal of resources, it can be considered the library's best acquisition. - Public, Two-Year School with between 2201 and 3500 students

The best purchases the library has ever made were ESCOE on-line internet access, and periodical literature. - Public, Two-Year School with between 2201 and 3500 students

The best purchase the library ever made was a teaching lab, which includes 11 computers, a projector, a printer, tables, and chairs. - Private, Four-Year School with between 2201 and 3500 students

The best purchase that the library ever made was the on-line system; it was a major change from the card file and people were really excited about it. - Public, Four-Year School with 7751 students or more

The best purchase the library has ever made was the Info Track database; it is easy to use and offers access to information in full-text format. - Public, Two-Year School with 2200 students or fewer

The best overall purchase that the library ever made was the integrated on-line system. - Private, Four-Year School with 7751 students or more

The best purchase the library has ever made was the CD-ROM index, Academic Abstracts; it has a combination of both common pop magazines and more advanced magazines and journals. - Public, Two-Year School with between 3501 and 7750 students

The library doesn't single out any one product as the best purchase its ever made, but says internet technology in general, holds that place. - Private, Four-Year School with 2200 students or fewer

The best purchase that the library has ever made was FirstSearch database. The library credits it with being inexpensive, good information, that's available in full-text immediately. - Public, Two-Year School with 2200 students or fewer

The best purchase the library ever made was Innovative Interfaces (Triple 'I'). "It really just does a good job, and it's easy to use." - Public, Two-Year School with between 2201 and 3500 students

The best purchase that the library has ever made was its first CD-ROM, SIRS, because of its full text. "As for other stuff," the library says, "our microfiche printer, because we have so much on microfiche--we'd probably just close down if we didn't have that. - Public, Two-Year School with 2200 students or fewer

The best purchase the library has ever made was videocassettes. The library is located in a small town in a remote, rural area; our students have few entertainment resources. Video movies, free via the library, have been a great boon for them. - Public, Two-Year School with between 2201 and 3500 students

No one thing comes to mind as the best purchase the library has ever made. - Public, Two-Year School with 2200 students or fewer

The best purchase the library has ever made was Lexis Nexus, because of its full-text and wider variety. We get Academic Universe--it's not the full Lexis Nexus, but except for the hard sciences it has everything, court cases, news, etc. - Public, Four-Year School with between 3501 and 7750

The best purchase that the library has ever made was Keynotes, the library's automated system. It's allowed us to get rid of the card catalogs and made the catalog accessible outside the library. It's been a lot better for both patrons and staff in aspects of service and administration. - Private, Four-Year School with between 3501 and 7750 students

The best purchase the library has ever made is access to the Omaha World Herald. Most students are in allied health and nursing and it's very useful for searching for health related articles. - Private, Four-Year School with 2200 students or fewer

The best purchase the library ever made was computer equipment for public works. - Public, Two-Year School with between 3501 and 7750 students

The best purchase the library ever made was going from terminals to PCs. - Public, Two-Year School with 7751 students or more

The best purchase the library ever made was newer computers, to replace the old. - Private, Four-Year School with between 3501 and 7750 students

The best purchase the library ever made was a network for reference databases, that connects all databases (CD-ROM network). - Public, Two-Year School with 7751 students or more

The best purchase the library ever made was it subscription to Carl. - Public, Two-Year School with between 3501 and 7750 students

The best purchase the library ever made was the inventory module for its on-line system, because it updated the inventory very easily. - Public, Two-Year School with between 3501 and 7750 students

The best purchase the library ever made was its on-line integrated catalog system. - Public, Two-Year School with 7751 students or more

The best purchase the library ever made was its own Sun server to manage access to on-line services.Private, Four-Year School with between 3501 and 7750 students

The best purchase the library ever made was an upgraded web-based catalog. It made a big difference; there's no more telnet stuff. - Public, Four-Year School with 7751 students or more

The best purchase the library has ever made was InfoTrack. Because of its full text, the library reports, patrons love it. - Public, Two-Year School with between 3501 and 7500 students

The best purchase the library ever made was computers and web-based resources. - Public, Two-Year School with 7751 students or more

The best purchase the library ever made was 2 CD-ROM towers for the NY Times and Sacramento Bee subscriptions that the library has. - Public, Two-Year School with 7751 students or more

The best purchase the library ever made was the integrated library software system, because when we put it in place, the usage of the entire library jumped 50% and remained high. - Private, Four-Year School with 2200 students or fewer

The best purchase the library ever made was UMI Proquest, because it's full-text and up to date--almost to the date. "We're very happy with it." - Private, Two-Year School with 7751 students or more

The best purchase the library ever made was a new building with 81 computers; it was a huge success. - Private, Four-Year School with between 3501 and 7750 students

What is the best single management idea adopted by your library, and why was it such a good idea, what did it accomplish?

As for the single best management idea, "unfortunately, I'm still looking for a way to optimize resources and service in a one-person, off-campus research center serving more than 200 faculty and staff." - Public, Four-Year School with 2200 students or less

The best single management idea adopted by the library was "studying, comparing, and adopting what is best for the campus, not what is on the market." - Private, Four-Year School with between 2201 and 3500 students

The best single management idea adopted by the library was "hiring a librarian with computer expertise; he can do most things we want done, or help us understand limitations and opportunities." - Public, Four-Year School with between 3501 and 7750 students

The single best management idea was "providing computers early and getting computer training for staff; this enabled staff to get a head start on the whole internet revolution and provide leadership to the campus." - Public, Four-Year School with 7751 students or more

The best management idea adopted by the library was "staff trainers which resulted in empowerment, which is essential to utilization of our evolving tools of the trade; train more, expect more, and train more again. We do as much or more than ARL libraries because we assume we do it and train ourselves accordingly." - Private, Four-Year School with between 2201 and 3500 students

The best management idea the library has had is departmental authority, which gave heads the right to make decisions and contributed to communication. - Public, Four-Year School with between 3501 and 7750 students

The best management idea was the Virtual Library of Virginia (VIVA), a state-wide consortium which gives the library the ability to access many commercial databases via the WWW. This would be prohibitively expensive alone, but affordable in a consortium. - Public, Four-Year School with 2200 students or fewer

The best management idea has been "to commit to integrating information technology throughout all operations in the library. We have set up independent application, file, and web servers, which enables local control, maintenance, and upgrading. This resulted in greater reliability and better response time. - Public, Four-Year School with 7751 students or more

The single best management idea adopted by the library was using the internet to access major university libraries to obtain cataloging information/records for free. - Public, Two-Year School with 7751 students or more

The single best management idea adopted by the library was bringing computers into the library, because it increased the amount of accessible information. - Public, Two-Year School with between 2201 and 3500 students

The single best management idea adopted by the library was creating joint technical services with a neighboring institution. It led to cooperative collection development, less duplication of technical service functions and a joint on-line catalog. - Private, Four-Year School with 2200 students or fewer

The single best management idea adopted by the library was forming a consortium with other libraries to share a single catalog and other searches, including document delivery. - Private, Four-Year School with between 3501 and 7750 students

The single best management idea adopted by the library was to "in general quit doing some functions and processes on the basis of 'well, we've always done that, and we've always done that a certain way.' The result was a change in thinking, approach, and participation." - Private, Four-Year School with 2200 students or fewer

The single best management idea used in this library was a commitment to cross-training all employees. It has made it possible to keep the library operating efficiently and well, despite inadequate staffing and long hours. - Public, Four-Year School with between 2201 and 3500 students

The single best management idea adopted by the library has been changing the circulation procedures for the special collection. We used to check them out for 4 weeks, but we've reduced that time. Now, we don't lose as much of the collection. We have a special collection of books by African-Americans, since we have so many classes that need these books, we lost a lot of them. - Private, Four-Year School with 2200 students or fewer

The single best management idea adopted by the library was putting everything on computer. - Public, Two-Year School with 2200 students or fewer

The single best management idea adopted by the library was to have workstations. - Private, Four-Year School with 7751 students or more

The single best management idea adopted by the library was instant document delivery or full-text databases. - Private, Four-Year School with 2200 students or fewer

The single best management idea adopted by the library was deciding to automate. - Public, Two-Year School with 2200 students or fewer

The single best management idea adopted by the library was decentralizing authority and flattening the hierarchy, which released the energy of the workers. - Public, Four-Year School with 7751 students or more

The single best management idea adopted by the library was getting access to the internet. It gave us access to resources far beyond the capabilities of a small, under-budgeted library. - Public, Two-Year School with between 2201 and 3500 students

The single best management idea adopted by the library was the reorganization of where we kept the computers and other machinery, like the microfilm readers, used by patrons; changing the layout of the library was the best management idea. - Public, Two-Year College with 2200 students or fewer

The single best management idea adopted by the library was creating a home page with links to sources, because we were having to remember too many things. With the bookmarks it's not so awkward--we're better organized. - Public, Four-Year School with between 3501 and 7750 students

The best management idea adopted by the library was making changes with the division secretary. The emphasis has changed with her now working with all departments to help with the work flow. - Public, Two-Year School with 7751 students or more

The best management idea adopted by the library was reorganizing positions. The library assigned positions different functions, taking the library more towards new technology. Specifically the circulation position was converted to a more technology-oriented position, this led to a decrease in books circulated. - Public, Two-Year School with between 3501 and 7750 students

The best management idea adopted by the library was changing the bottom floor, creating a ready reference section and putting in 25 new computers. - Public, Two-Year School with between 3501 and 7750 students

The single best management idea adopted by the library was empowering individual departments and bringing technology to everyone. - Public, Two-Year School with 7751 students or more

The best management idea adopted by the library was combining media services with the library systems computing under one manager. - Private, Four-Year School with between 3501 and 7750 students

The best management idea adopted by the library was hiring 2 replacement librarian positions. It led to a greater emphasis being put on public services. Now, one position is responsible for outreach and marketing, and one position is in charge of circulation and technical services. These changes led to remarkable differences in efficiency. - Public, Two-Year School with 7751 students or more

The best management idea adopted by the library was giving the library on-line access. Its ease of use made the biggest difference. - Public, Two-Year School with 7751 students or more

The best management idea adopted by the library was the integration between library and computer center services. - Private, Four-Year School with between 2201 and 3500 students

The single best management idea adopted by the library was to move from a library staff that was para-professionally based to a professionally based one. We went from one professional librarian on a staff of ten, to seven professional librarians on a staff of ten. - Private, Four-Year School with 2200 students or fewer

The single best management idea adopted by the library was teamwork. - Private, Two-Year School with 7751 students or more

The single best management idea adopted by the library was going from a very traditional job hierarchy structure with a dean, to having 2 chairs (directors) overseeing 2 libraries. - Private, Four-Year School with between 3501 and 7750 students

We are joining OhioLink. It's in the process. It's a shared catalog of all academic libraries in Ohio. Private institutions, like us, have to pay. The state pays for public schools, at least to start. - Private, Four-Year School with 2200 students or fewer

We did a reorganization that brought acquisitions and technical services together. It was a good idea because it streamlined acquisitions processes and enabled us to outsource. - Public, Four-Year School with 7751 students or more

FirstSearch, because it has so much available under the same search strategy, it has the same interface for so many different databases. - Private, Four-Year School with between 2201 and 3500 students

Outsourcing, definitely without a doubt the way to go, with a small community college with a small book budget. - Public, Two-Year School with 7751 students or more

Basically it was creating committees and task forces to have people that were actually carrying out the decisions. So, involving the staff at all their different levels in the library wide decisions, has been the best management idea. - Public, Four-Year School with between 3501 and 7750 students

The jobs the staff does are always changing. Two professionals are going off campus to receive some training. - Public, Two-Year School with between 2201 and 3500 students

To change management, because the working environment had to be improved. - Public, Four-Year School with 7751 students or more

To centralize purchasing for the campus library and two extension centers. - Public, Two-Year School with between 2201 and 3500 students

Changing the library director and moving people around. - Private, Four-Year School with between 3501 and 7750 students

Splitting the library and computer budget up. They had nothing in common budgetarily, so they have now become separate entities with their own administration and budget. - Private, Four-Year School with 2200 students or fewer

Planning; you don't do things in a vacuum, you really define what you do, and who are our customers? What are the results? How are these planned? Systematic planning is very rare in academic environments. - Private, Four-Year School with 2200 students or fewer

No significant changes. Just following trends like: we created a Copyright Department and a Digital Imaging Department. - Private, Four-Year School with 7751 students or more

Frequent communication between the director and the staff. Whatever idea I have, I talk to my staff. We don't have regular meetings, but I just go and talk to them. Hands on management. It helps to better serve our patrons. Whatever problems patrons have, it gets fixed right away, library's are based on service. - Public, Two-Year School with between 3501 and 7750 students

An on-line catalog consisting of 38 Community Colleges. Students can search for info. and request it from one of the 38 schools that are participating. - Public, Two-Year School with between 2201 and 3500 students

To automate the library. - Public, Two-Year School with between 3501 and 7750 students

Participatory management. I mean when the library director is not a dictator, lording his power over his colleagues. - Private, Four-Year School with between 2201 and 3500 students

Anticipating hiring student workers with computer knowledge. - Private, Four-Year School with between 2201 and 3500 students

To divide the duties of the technical services personnel, because I think the technical services have to be really efficient. It just helps us facilitate things better. - Private, Four-Year School with 2200 students or less

Were going to purchase a print manager program. Well, the way it is right now, if you want to photograph it costs a nickel. But, if it's printed off the internet it's free. This new system means that the copies are gonna have to be paid for. We're going to charge students for printing out stuff off the internet. A nickel a page.

It'll save paper and reimburse us for what we're paying for the paper. Recently, we had two girls come in and print out about 1,000 pages worth of quilting patterns in over 3 days. - Public, Two-Year School with between 3501 and 7750 students

Regional consortium made tremendous impact on cooperation between libraries. - Private, Four-Year School with between 2201 and 3500 students

Information technology internet access, through common browser interface, it's made a huge difference and has been highly beneficial. - Public, Four-Year School with 7751 students or more

APPENDIX B: OTHER REPORTS AVAILABLE FROM PRIMARY RESEARCH GROUP

The Survey of College Marketing Programs
Publication Date: October 1998

This special survey report from Primary Research Group will present detailed data, broken out by size and type of school, for marketing expenditures and practices of American and Canadian colleges and universities. Answer questions such as: What percentage of American colleges present a CD-ROM to potential applicants? What percentage of community colleges plan to develop a CD-ROM? What percentage of private colleges? How much do they spend per new incoming student on their viewbooks, radio advertising, sponsored campus visits? What percentage of their applications do they receive on-line? Hundreds of tables of useful data conveniently broken out by size and type of institution of higher education.

Enrollment Growth Data Report (isbn#: 1-57440-013-4)
(price: $75.00) Publication Date: July 1998

This report gives programs administrators the tools to help predict enrollment growth for the Nation, as well as their city, state or region. In addition to suggesting forecasting methodologies and demonstrating their use, the report gives nuts and bolts data on student and enrollment growth rates, and rates of growth of variables that impact enrollment growth.

Corporate/Government Use of Distance Learning (isbn#: 1-57440-014-2)
(price: $110.00) Publication Date: July 1998

This special report from Primary Research Group demonstrates how prestigious corporations and government agencies use distance learning in their training programs.

How to Estimate the Local, Regional and National Markets for Employer-Paid Tuition
(isbn#: 1-57440-012-6)
(price: $85.00) Publication Date: June 1998

This special report gives advice to colleges on how to estimate the local, regional and national market for college courses paid for by employers. By using data available from publicly available sources, this monograph shows how - at virtually no or very little cost - to estimate the extent of demand for college courses that are paid for by employers in particular states, municipalities or counties.

Corporate/Government Partnerships with Higher Education in Training and Human Resource Development (isbn#: 1-57440-012-6)
(Price: $97.50) Publication Date: June 1998

This special report looks closely at how institutions of higher education and corporate and government training and human resource departments are cooperating to lower costs and improve quality in corporate training and employee recruitment and development programs.

Primary Research Group, Inc.   **68 W. 38th St., #202, NY, NY 10018**   **(212)764-1579**

Evaluating the College: Performance Assessment in Higher Education (isbn#: 1-57440-010)
(Price: $57.50) Published in March 1997

This report looks closely at how the Nation's colleges and universities evaluate themselves, and how they are evaluated by federal and state agencies, education consulting firms and oversight bodies, the media, corporations, and students.

Profiles of College and University Distance Learning Programs (isbn#: 1-57440-009-6)
(Price: $80.00) Published in February 1998

This report enables administrators of distance education programs to share the distance learning "war stories" of program directors across North America. The study furnishes useful insights into a myriad of difficult choices including technology acquisition, selection of course offerings, approaches to the industrial training market, and ways of dealing with often suspicious traditional faculty members.

The Adult and Continuing Education Business Report (isbn#: 1-57440-007-X)
(Price: $295.00/$95.00 for accredited academic institutions) Published in October 1997

This special report looks closely at trends in adult and continuing education in the United States, imparting essential planning information for strategic development. The report helps administrators to forecast the best areas for future growth, and forecast general trends in adult education spending. Profiles college and private sector adult education programs. Gives market demographic data on who takes what kind of adult education classes.

The Survey of Distance Learning Programs in Higher Education (isbn#: 1-57440-008-8)
(Price $85.00) Published in October 1997

This special report - based on survey data from college and university distance learning programs in the United States and Canada - gives higher education administrators hard data to make decisions on the financing, scope, and development of distance learning efforts. It presents findings on: the cost of distance learning programs; faculty compensation and organization; student demographics; technology; course development; and administrative organization and office politics.

Restructuring Higher Education: Cost Containment and Productivity Enhancement Efforts of North American Colleges and Universities (isbn# 1-57440-006-1)
(Price: $59.50) Published in June 1997

This monograph looks closely at the cost containment and restructuring efforts of North American colleges and universities. Among the many issues discussed: trends in the employment of adjuncts, departmental reorganizations, use of new technologies such as advanced database software and the internet, the politics of administrative downsizing, cooperation among colleges to enhance bargaining power with suppliers in purchasing, "performance contracting", electric power procurement, telecommunications services procurement, "speeded-up" three-year degrees, outsourcing of student services such as food service and residence halls, and many other issues of interest to college administrators.

Primary Research Group, Inc.   **68 W. 38th St., #202, NY, NY 10018**   **(212)764-1579**

Forecasting College and University Revenues (isbn#: 1-57440-003-7)
(Price: $130.00/$65.00 for accredited educational institutions) Published in April 1997

This special report examines the income outlook for American colleges and universities, exploring trends in overall enrollment, tuition, licensing, and endowment income, for profit college services, foreign student enrollment, state local and federal government support, and research income. Includes time series data on US consumer spending for higher education over the past 15 years.

The Academic Library Budget & Expenditure Report (isbn#: 1-57440-027-4)
(Price: $125.00/$70.00 for accredited educational institutions) Published in October 1996

This special report is designed to give academic librarians insight into the materials and technology purchasing plans of America's two-year, four-year and university academic libraries. The data in the report is based on 100 randomly chosen academic libraries in North America; data is presented on a per student basis, as well as in the aggregate, and broken out by size and type of library to allow for easy benchmarking and comparisons. Among the data categories: spending for journals, cataloging systems, CD-ROM, computer hardware, online services, books, salaries, etc. Also explores issues such as personnel benefits, internet usage patterns, seminar attendance and other issues of interest to academic librarians.

Primary Research Group, Inc.   **68 W. 38th St., #202, NY, NY 10018**   **(212)764-1579**